contents

Key

Number and Place value

Addition and Subtraction

Multiplication and Division

Shape and Measure

Fractions

Mixed Operations

How to use this book

Your teacher may tell you to GRAB something that might help you answer the questions.

The first page of each section will have a title telling you what the next few pages are about.

Read the instructions carefully before each set of questions.

Sometimes a character will give you a tip.

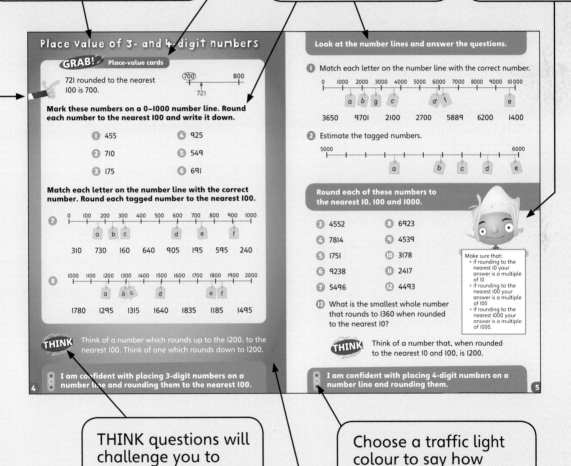

THINK questions will challenge you to think more about the maths on the page.

Choose a traffic light colour to say how confident you are with the maths on the page.

Some pages will show you an example or model.

Each area of maths has its own colour.

Place-value cards

721 rounded to the nearest 100 is 700.

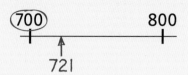

Mark these numbers on a 0–1000 number line. Round each number to the nearest 100 and write it down.

1 455

4 925

2 710

5 549

3 175

6 691

Match each letter on the number line with the correct number. Round each tagged number to the nearest 100.

7

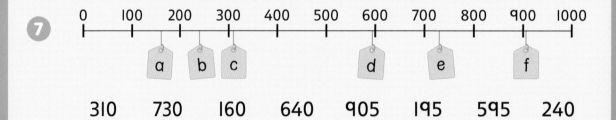

310   730   160   640   905   195   595   240

8

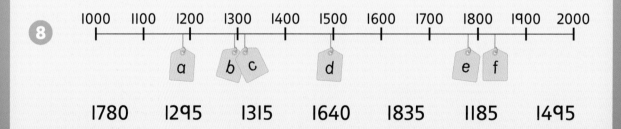

1780   1295   1315   1640   1835   1185   1495

THINK Think of a number which rounds up to 1200, to the nearest 100. Think of one which rounds down to 1200.

○
○ **I am confident with placing 3-digit numbers on a**
○ **number line and rounding them to the nearest 100.**

4

1 Match each letter on the number line with the correct number.

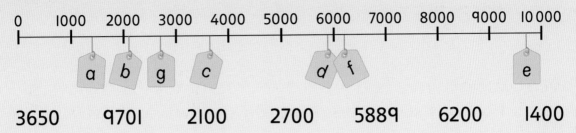

3650   9701   2100   2700   5889   6200   1400

2 Estimate the tagged numbers.

Round each of these numbers to the nearest 10, 100 and 1000.

3 4552

4 7814

5 1751

6 9238

7 5496

8 6923

9 4539

10 3178

11 2417

12 4493

Make sure that:
- if rounding to the nearest 10 your answer is a multiple of 10
- if rounding to the nearest 100 your answer is a multiple of 100
- if rounding to the nearest 1000 your answer is a multiple of 1000.

13 What is the smallest whole number that rounds to 1360 when rounded to the nearest 10?

 **THINK** Think of a number that, when rounded to the nearest 10 and 100, is 1200.

I am confident with placing 4-digit numbers on a number line and rounding them.

1. The height of the mountain Ben Lawers is 1214 m. Ben Nevis is 130 m taller. What is the height of Ben Nevis?

2. In Africa, Mount Auasberge is 2485 m high. In Wales, the height of Mount Snowdon is 1400 m less than this. How high is Snowdon?

3. The highest mountain in the world, Everest, is 8848 m. The highest mountain in the Alps, Mont Blanc, is 4041 m shorter. How high is Mont Blanc?

4. Charles Dickens wrote *Oliver Twist* in 1838. 160 years later, JK Rowling's book *Harry Potter and the Chamber of Secrets* was published. What year was that?

5. William Shakespeare was born in 1564. When he was 35 years old, the Globe theatre was built. What year was this?

6. The Battle of Hastings took place in 1066. The battle of the Spanish Armada was 522 years later. When was that?

7. On Monday, 845 people clicked on a website to buy tickets for a concert. On Tuesday, the number of people who clicked on it was 1030 more than on Monday. How many people clicked on the website on Tuesday?

8. A website had 3562 hits during the year 2012. During 2013 it had 3007 more hits. How many hits did it have in 2013?

 Write your own problem for 4726 – 2010.

I am confident with mentally solving additions and subtractions using place value.

Start at 1008. Write the next ten numbers in the sequence:

Estimate where you will get to with each count before you do it!

1. counting on in 25s.

2. counting on in 50s.

3. counting on in 100s.

4. Which numbers appear in all three sequences?

5. Predict another five numbers that would appear in all three sequences if you were to continue counting on.

THINK Describe the pattern in the units when counting on in 25s.

Start at 4446. Write the next ten numbers in the sequence:

6. counting back in 25s.

7. counting back in 50s.

8. counting back in 100s.

9. Which numbers appear in all three sequences?

10. Find three more numbers that will appear in all three sequences if you continue counting back.

THINK Describe the pattern in the units when counting back in 25s.

I am confident with counting on and back from a given number in steps of 25, 50 and 100 and recognising patterns.

Add and subtract multiples of 10 and 100

Complete these additions.

1. 5673 + 20 = ☐

8. 3562 + 600 = ☐

2. 9663 + 300 = ☐

9. 7894 + 30 = ☐

3. 3456 + 40 = ☐

10. 1353 + 800 = ☐

4. 5138 + 600 = ☐

11. 6875 + 50 = ☐

5. 6835 + 50 = ☐

12. 8254 + 900 = ☐

6. 8392 + 500 = ☐

13. 2442 + 80 = ☐

7. 5251 + 50 = ☐

14. 2847 + 800 = ☐

Remember to add the 10s and then add the 100s.

15. 4860 + 120 = ☐

19. 2578 + 420 = ☐

16. 7574 + 320 = ☐

20. 7858 + 140 = ☐

17. 2385 + 510 = ☐

21. 6684 + 130 = ☐

18. 5273 + 710 = ☐

22. 2329 + 560 = ☐

 Look at the questions. Find one which was a 'no work' place-value addition. Now find one which was harder. Why was it harder?

I am confident with adding multiples of 10 and 100 to 4-digit numbers.

Complete these additions.

1 5788 + 60 = ☐

2 4673 + 500 = ☐

3 1265 + 70 = ☐

4 5918 + 500 = ☐

5 9254 + 50 = ☐

6 3268 + 700 = ☐

7 2393 + 800 = ☐

8 6735 + 90 = ☐

9 2586 + 600 = ☐

10 9024 + 80 = ☐

11 3962 + 400 = ☐

12 4667 + 80 = ☐

Remember to add the 10s and then add the 100s.

13 4860 + 320 = ☐

14 7574 + 250 = ☐

15 2395 + 520 = ☐

16 5673 + 710 = ☐

17 2578 + 650 = ☐

18 7858 + 360 = ☐

19 6674 + 640 = ☐

20 2639 + 580 = ☐

Write a 'no work' place-value 4-digit + 3-digit addition.

Write another 4-digit + 3-digit addition where you must add the 10s and the 100s.

Complete these additions.

1. 5918 + 530 = ☐
2. 8654 + 670 = ☐
3. 4673 + 580 = ☐
4. 6547 + 280 = ☐
5. 1265 + 870 = ☐
6. 3268 + 750 = ☐
7. 1265 + 940 = ☐
8. 5788 + 630 = ☐
9. 7435 + 780 = ☐
10. 5665 + 540 = ☐

11. 2334 + 890 = ☐
12. 3962 + 480 = ☐
13. 6735 + 390 = ☐
14. 6846 + 470 = ☐
15. 2586 + 640 = ☐
16. 4667 + 820 = ☐
17. 3454 + 650 = ☐
18. 2393 + 810 = ☐
19. 5565 + 840 = ☐
20. 9724 + 870 = ☐

Solve these problems.

21. Which year falls 270 years after 1809?

22. Amy has £3675 in a bank account. She pays in £270 more. How much does she have now?

23. In a football stadium there are 4527 adults and 680 children. How many people altogether?

THINK

Start at 2643. How many times do you think you would add 340 before you pass 10 000? Now work it out. Were you right?

I am confident with adding multiples of 10 and 100 to 4-digit numbers.

Complete these subtractions.

1. 3456 − 40 = ☐
2. 5198 − 60 = ☐
3. 5251 − 50 = ☐
4. 6835 − 20 = ☐
5. 8663 − 30 = ☐
6. 8382 − 60 = ☐
7. 5643 − 50 = ☐
8. 4820 − 50 = ☐
9. 7574 − 300 = ☐
10. 2685 − 500 = ☐
11. 1353 − 300 = ☐
12. 6875 − 500 = ☐
13. 2847 − 800 = ☐
14. 8554 − 300 = ☐
15. 7294 − 400 = ☐
16. 2142 − 800 = ☐
17. 2654 − 320 = ☐
18. 2578 − 410 = ☐
19. 8858 − 640 = ☐
20. 6794 − 760 = ☐

Joe's mum was born in 1982. Write which year was:

21. 30 years before 1982.

22. 100 years before 1982.

23. 150 years before 1982.

 **THINK** Ed is playing a computer game. His score is 1317 until he begins landing on penalties of 100. How many can he land on before it is 'Game Over'?

I am confident with subtracting multiples of 10 and 100 from 4-digit numbers.

Complete these subtractions.

1. 5251 – 500 = ☐
2. 6382 – 60 = ☐
3. 3420 – 700 = ☐
4. 7574 – 800 = ☐
5. 5643 – 50 = ☐
6. 3456 – 90 = ☐
7. 5198 – 600 = ☐
8. 8663 – 90 = ☐
9. 2585 – 500 = ☐
10. 6835 – 40 = ☐

11. 1747 – 800 = ☐
12. 2142 – 70 = ☐
13. 2578 – 340 = ☐
14. 8858 – 450 = ☐
15. 2654 – 440 = ☐
16. 6353 – 340 = ☐
17. 3875 – 520 = ☐
18. 7694 – 470 = ☐
19. 6934 – 760 = ☐
20. 5827 – 490 = ☐

Avril's grandma was born in 1962. Write which year was:

21. 60 years before 1962.

22. 150 years before 1962.

23. 180 years before 1962.

 **THINK** Start at 248. How many 100s will you have to count back to reach 48? How many 10s will you have to count back to reach 48?

I am confident with subtracting multiples of 10 and 100 from 4-digit numbers.

Subtracting 3-digit numbers

GRAB!   Place-value cards

$$325 - 283 = 42$$

```
      200   120
      300    20    5
   -  200    80    3
      ────────────
             40    2
```

Perform the subtractions using the method shown.

1   655 – 338 = ☐

```
      600    50    5
   -  300    30    8
      ────────────
```

2   752 – 314 = ☐   **8**   962 – 354 = ☐

3   857 – 473 = ☐   **9**   855 – 726 = ☐

4   528 – 382 = ☐   **10**   775 – 291 = ☐

5   846 – 729 = ☐   **11**   663 – 472 = ☐

6   456 – 371 = ☐   **12**   956 – 366 = ☐

7   683 – 327 = ☐   **13**   456 – 248 = ☐

THINK   Choose three of the subtractions on the page to check using Frog.

○
○ **I am confident with column subtraction of 3-digit**
○ **numbers using the expanded method.**

13

Perform these subtractions using first the expanded and then the compact method.

$$\begin{array}{r} 537 \\ -\ 274 \\ \hline \end{array}$$

$$\begin{array}{r r r} 400 & 130 & \\ \cancel{500} & \cancel{30} & 7 \\ -\ 200 & 70 & 4 \\ \hline 200 & 60 & 3 \end{array}$$

$$\begin{array}{r} 4\ \ 13 \\ \cancel{5}\ \cancel{3}\ 7 \\ -\ 2\ 7\ 4 \\ \hline 2\ 6\ 3 \end{array}$$

1
$$\begin{array}{r} 864 \\ -\ 439 \\ \hline \end{array}$$

2
$$\begin{array}{r} 951 \\ -\ 647 \\ \hline \end{array}$$

3
$$\begin{array}{r} 928 \\ -\ 265 \\ \hline \end{array}$$

4
$$\begin{array}{r} 747 \\ -\ 365 \\ \hline \end{array}$$

Use either the expanded or compact method to perform these subtractions.

5
$$\begin{array}{r} 673 \\ -\ 338 \\ \hline \end{array}$$

8
$$\begin{array}{r} 962 \\ -\ 348 \\ \hline \end{array}$$

11
$$\begin{array}{r} 629 \\ -\ 271 \\ \hline \end{array}$$

14
$$\begin{array}{r} 546 \\ -\ 165 \\ \hline \end{array}$$

6
$$\begin{array}{r} 757 \\ -\ 639 \\ \hline \end{array}$$

9
$$\begin{array}{r} 658 \\ -\ 477 \\ \hline \end{array}$$

12
$$\begin{array}{r} 836 \\ -\ 256 \\ \hline \end{array}$$

15
$$\begin{array}{r} 752 \\ -\ 238 \\ \hline \end{array}$$

7
$$\begin{array}{r} 562 \\ -\ 353 \\ \hline \end{array}$$

10
$$\begin{array}{r} 871 \\ -\ 467 \\ \hline \end{array}$$

13
$$\begin{array}{r} 907 \\ -\ 473 \\ \hline \end{array}$$

16
$$\begin{array}{r} 888 \\ -\ 379 \\ \hline \end{array}$$

THINK Choose two subtractions from the page to check using Frog. Choose two others to check using addition.

I am confident with column subtraction of 3-digit numbers.

Perform these subtractions using the method shown.

$795 - 458 = 337$

		80	15
	700	~~90~~	~~5~~
−	400	50	8
	300	30	7

1 $569 - 475 = \square$

2 $438 - 264 = \square$

3 $875 - 348 = \square$

4 $956 - 849 = \square$

THINK Choose two of these subtractions to check using Frog.

Perform these subtractions.

5 $678 - 85 = \square$

6 $724 - 83 = \square$

7 $875 - 69 = \square$

8 $964 - 45 = \square$

9 $835 - 28 = \square$

10 $956 - 84 = \square$

THINK Choose two of these subtractions to check using addition.

Solve these problems.

11 There are 327 people at a football match. Of them, 64 are children. How many are adults?

12 A male African elephant is 364 cm tall. A female elephant is 72 cm shorter. How tall is she?

I am confident with column subtraction of 2-digit and 3-digit numbers using the expanded method.

15

Perform these subtractions using the method shown.

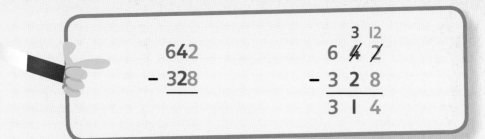

$$
\begin{array}{r}
642 \\
- 328 \\
\hline
\end{array}
\qquad
\begin{array}{r}
^{3}\;^{12} \\
6\;\cancel{4}\;\cancel{2} \\
-\;3\;2\;8 \\
\hline
3\;1\;4 \\
\end{array}
$$

(1)
$$
\begin{array}{r}
753 \\
- 439 \\
\hline
\end{array}
$$

(2)
$$
\begin{array}{r}
842 \\
- 617 \\
\hline
\end{array}
$$

(3)
$$
\begin{array}{r}
817 \\
- 376 \\
\hline
\end{array}
$$

(4)
$$
\begin{array}{r}
676 \\
- 481 \\
\hline
\end{array}
$$

 Choose two of these subtractions to check using Frog.

Use the same method to perform these.

(5)
$$
\begin{array}{r}
782 \\
- \;\;58 \\
\hline
\end{array}
$$

(7)
$$
\begin{array}{r}
851 \\
- \;\;48 \\
\hline
\end{array}
$$

(9)
$$
\begin{array}{r}
718 \\
- \;\;62 \\
\hline
\end{array}
$$

(11)
$$
\begin{array}{r}
657 \\
- \;\;85 \\
\hline
\end{array}
$$

(6)
$$
\begin{array}{r}
673 \\
- \;\;37 \\
\hline
\end{array}
$$

(8)
$$
\begin{array}{r}
982 \\
- \;\;91 \\
\hline
\end{array}
$$

(10)
$$
\begin{array}{r}
666 \\
- \;\;48 \\
\hline
\end{array}
$$

(12)
$$
\begin{array}{r}
778 \\
- \;\;59 \\
\hline
\end{array}
$$

 Choose two of these subtractions to check using addition.

Work out what number is:

(13) 84 less than 638.

(14) 79 less than 419.

 What is the smallest number you can subtract from 321 to give a 2-digit number as an answer?

I am confident with column subtraction of 2-digit and 3-digit numbers using the compact method.

16

Perform these subtractions using the compact column method.

1
```
   578
 − 489
```

3
```
   944
 − 687
```

5
```
   625
 − 376
```

7
```
   836
 − 287
```

2
```
   713
 − 439
```

4
```
   814
 − 638
```

6
```
   817
 − 379
```

8
```
   683
 − 389
```

Use the same method to perform these.

9
```
   784
 −  58
```

11
```
   871
 −  68
```

13
```
   718
 −  69
```

15
```
   653
 −  85
```

10
```
   542
 −  91
```

12
```
   952
 −  86
```

14
```
   533
 −  78
```

16
```
   964
 −  87
```

Solve these problems.

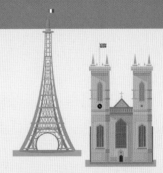

17 The Eiffel Tower is 324 m tall. Westminster Abbey is only 68 m tall. What is the difference between the two heights?

18 A laptop costing £649 is reduced in price by £88. How much does it cost now?

```
5  4  5  −  ☐  ☐  9  =  1  ☐  6
```

What could the missing numbers be?
How many possible solutions are there?

○
○ **I am confident with column subtraction of 2-digit**
○ **and 3-digit numbers using the compact method.**

Multiplying 3-digit numbers by 1-digit numbers

Remember to leave space for any digits moved across in the addition!

```
  346        346
×   4      ×   4
           1200 ←— 4 × 300
            160 ←— 4 ×  40
          +  24 ←— 4 ×   6
          _____
           1384
```

Use the ladder method to perform these multiplications.

1	724 × 3		5	786 × 6		9	756 × 8
2	457 × 5		6	977 × 4		10	369 × 6
3	683 × 4		7	867 × 3		11	877 × 8
4	458 × 3		8	349 × 6		12	389 × 6

 **THINK** Which multiplication did you find the quickest? Which one took the longest? Why do you think this was?

○ **I am confident with multiplying 3-digit numbers by**
○ **1-digit numbers using the ladder method.**

Use the ladder method to perform these multiplications.

1   337
   ×   6
___

4   776
   ×   8
___

7   888
   ×   8
___

2   779
   ×   4
___

5   669
   ×   3
___

8   836
   ×   6
___

3   987
   ×   8
___

6   889
   ×   6
___

9   379
   ×   8
___

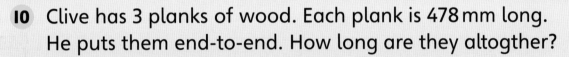

Solve these problems using the same method.

10 Clive has 3 planks of wood. Each plank is 478 mm long. He puts them end-to-end. How long are they altogther?

11 There are 578 sheep in a field. How many legs?

12 Each box holds 256 paper clips. How many paper clips in 5 boxes?

13 During one week, a truck driver travels 367 km each weekday (Monday to Friday). How far does he travel altogether?

14 A machine makes 456 bottles in one minute. How many does it make in 8 minutes?

15 Lauren pays 6p per minute for phone calls. How much does she pay for 156 minutes?

 **THINK**   Multiply 999 by 2, by 3 and by 4?
What do you notice about the answers?

I am confident with multiplying 3-digit numbers by 1-digit numbers using the ladder method.

Use the grid method to perform these multiplications.

4 × £4·23

×	£4	20p	3p
4	£16	80p	12p

= ☐

How much will you spend if you buy 4 of each of these?

1  £4·23

2  £5·39

3  £7·86

How much will you spend if you buy 6 of each of these?

4  £6·59

5  £8·36

6  £3·68

How much will you spend if you buy 8 of each of these?

7  £3·66

8 £4·87

9  £2·59

THINK

×			
3	£9	60p	12p

= £9·72

○
○ I am confident with multiplying amounts of money
○ by 1-digit numbers.

You have £30 to spend. Find as many combinations of these as you can buy.

Jigsaw puzzles cost £4·39. Board games cost £7·25.
You must buy at least one puzzle and one board game.

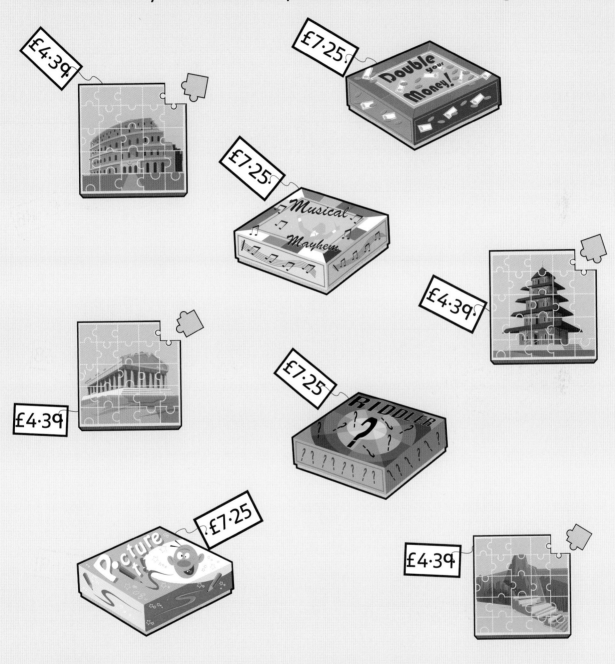

£4·39

£7·25

£7·25

£4·39

£4·39

£7·25

£7·25

£4·39

THINK Which of the combinations you have found gives the smallest amount of change from £30?

I am confident with multiplying amounts of money by 1-digit numbers.

Work out the outputs for these function machines.

34 [× 2] = 68 ⟶ [× 2] = 136 ⟶ 34 × 4 = 136

1   46 [× 2] = ☐ ⟶ [× 2] = ☐ ⟶ 46 × 4 = ☐

2   72 [× 2] = ☐ ⟶ [× 2] = ☐ ⟶ 72 × 4 = ☐

3   26 [× 2] ☐ ⟶ [×10] ☐ ⟶ 26 × 20 = ☐

4   84 [× 2] ☐ ⟶ [×10] ☐ ⟶ 84 × 20 = ☐

5   78 [× 2] ☐ ⟶ [×10] ☐ ⟶ 78 × 20 = ☐

6   44 [×10] ☐ ⟶ [÷ 2] ☐ ⟶ 44 × 5 = ☐

7   68 [×10] ☐ ⟶ [÷ 2] ☐ ⟶ 68 × 5 = ☐

8   74 [×10] ☐ ⟶ [÷ 2] ☐ ⟶ 74 × 5 = ☐

THINK   48 came out of this machine. How do you work out what went in?

☐ [× 2] ⟶ [× 2] = 48

● ○ ○   **I am confident with multiplying 2-digit numbers by 4, 5 and 20 using mental methods.**

Multiply these numbers by 4, using the two machines shown.

1 46   **4** 424

2 57   **5** 326

3 312

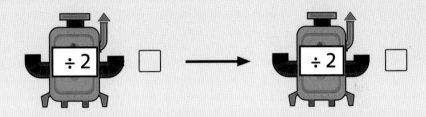

Divide these numbers by 4, using the two machines shown.

6 64   **9** 636

7 124   **10** 812

8 316

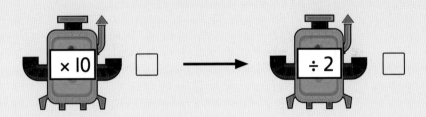

Multiply these numbers by 5, using the two machines shown.

11 46   **14** 861

12 57   **15** 354

13 312

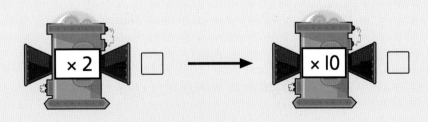

Multiply these numbers by 20, using the two machines shown.

16 46   **19** 474

17 57   **20** 745

18 312

 **THINK** Draw a function machine which divides by 20 in two stages.

I am confident with multiplying 2-digit and 3-digit numbers by 4, 5 and 20 and dividing numbers by 4 using mental methods.

23

Calculate the answers.

1 $35 \times 4 = \square$

2 $68 \times 4 = \square$

3 $128 \div 4 = \square$

4 $436 \div 4 = \square$

5 $76 \times 4 = \square$

6 $4 \times 158 = \square$

7 $308 \div 4 = \square$

8 $112 \div 4 = \square$

9 $135 \times 4 = \square$

10 $688 \div 4 = \square$

Solve these problems.

11 How many horseshoes are needed for 73 horses?

12 A machine fits wheels onto new cars in a factory. It fits 4 wheels per car. How many cars can have wheels if there are 648 wheels?

13 The 4 boys in the Smith family are given £364 to share equally between them. How much does each boy get?

14 How many tins of beans in 123 packs of 4 tins?

15 Lia pays 4p per minute for phone calls. She pays £2·32 for calls. How many minutes is this?

16 For a pancake recipe Mrs Patel needs 145 g of flour per person. How many grams of flour does she need for 4 people?

 **THINK** Write your own problem for $66 \times 4 = \square$.

I am confident with multiplying and dividing 2-digit and 3-digit numbers by 4 using mental methods.

Finding non-unit fractions of 2- and 3-digit numbers

Find the answers in each pair.

1. $\frac{1}{4}$ of 16 = ☐ ⟶ $\frac{3}{4}$ of 16 = ☐

2. $\frac{1}{3}$ of 15 = ☐ ⟶ $\frac{2}{3}$ of 15 = ☐

3. $\frac{1}{6}$ of 66 = ☐ ⟶ $\frac{5}{6}$ of 66 = ☐

4. $\frac{1}{8}$ of 160 = ☐ ⟶ $\frac{3}{8}$ of 160 = ☐

5. $\frac{1}{9}$ of 45 = ☐ ⟶ $\frac{8}{9}$ of 45 = ☐

6. $\frac{1}{7}$ of 42 = ☐ ⟶ $\frac{3}{7}$ of 42 = ☐

7. $\frac{1}{9}$ of 27 = ☐ ⟶ $\frac{4}{9}$ of 27 = ☐

8. $\frac{1}{100}$ of 500 = ☐ ⟶ $\frac{3}{100}$ of 500 = ☐

9. $\frac{1}{10}$ of 300 = ☐ ⟶ $\frac{3}{10}$ of 300 = ☐

> Remember to find $\frac{1}{4}$, $\frac{1}{5}$ or $\frac{1}{10}$ first.

Find these fractions.

10. $\frac{3}{4}$ of 12 = ☐

11. $\frac{4}{5}$ of 30 = ☐

12. $\frac{7}{10}$ of 40 = ☐

13. $\frac{2}{5}$ of 55 = ☐

THINK Find $\frac{1}{3}$ and $\frac{2}{3}$ of 12, 24, 36, 48, 60, 72. Describe the patterns that you notice.

○○○ **I am confident with finding unit and non-unit fractions of amounts.**

Find these pairs of fractions.

1 $\frac{1}{3}$ of 60 = ☐

$\frac{2}{3}$ of 60 = ☐

2 $\frac{1}{5}$ of 60 = ☐

$\frac{4}{5}$ of 60 = ☐

3 $\frac{1}{7}$ of 140 = ☐

$\frac{3}{7}$ of 140 = ☐

4 $\frac{1}{6}$ of 120 = ☐

$\frac{5}{6}$ of 120 = ☐

5 $\frac{1}{10}$ of 500 = ☐

$\frac{7}{10}$ of 500 = ☐

> Use your answer to the first of each pair to help you answer the second.

6 $\frac{1}{100}$ of 600 = ☐

$\frac{3}{100}$ of 600 = ☐

7 $\frac{1}{4}$ of 160 = ☐

$\frac{3}{4}$ of 160 = ☐

8 $\frac{1}{4}$ of 800 = ☐

$\frac{3}{4}$ of 800 = ☐

9 $\frac{1}{10}$ of 70 = ☐

$\frac{9}{10}$ of 70 = ☐

10 $\frac{1}{7}$ of 49 = ☐

$\frac{4}{7}$ of 49 = ☐

A school has 252 pupils and 9 classes.
Each class has the same number of pupils.

11 What fraction of the whole school are 2 classes?

12 What fraction of the whole school are 7 classes?

13 How many children are in 5 classes?

14 Half of the children in one class are 7-year-old girls.
If there are no other 7-year-old girls in the school,
what fraction of the school are 7-year-old girls?

 **THINK** If $\frac{1}{7}$ of a number is between 35 and 40, and $\frac{2}{7}$ of the

number is ☐4, what is the number? What is $\frac{6}{7}$ of it?

○
○ **I am confident with finding unit and non-unit**
○ **fractions of amounts.**

Find these fractions.

Remember to find the unit fraction first for questions 5-12.

① $\frac{1}{4}$ of 200 = ☐

$\frac{3}{4}$ of 200 = ☐

② $\frac{1}{5}$ of 500 = ☐

$\frac{3}{5}$ of 500 = ☐

③ $\frac{1}{6}$ of 240 = ☐

$\frac{5}{6}$ of 240 = ☐

④ $\frac{1}{5}$ of 150 = ☐

$\frac{4}{5}$ of 150 = ☐

⑤ $\frac{3}{8}$ of 88 = ☐

⑥ $\frac{3}{7}$ of 140 = ☐

⑦ $\frac{3}{10}$ of 200 = ☐

⑧ $\frac{13}{100}$ of 400 = ☐

⑨ $\frac{5}{8}$ of 160 = ☐

⑩ $\frac{2}{3}$ of 180 = ☐

⑪ $\frac{5}{7}$ of 77 = ☐

⑫ $\frac{2}{5}$ of 400 = ☐

I am a number. Who am I?

⑬ I am one-half of a fifth of 20.

⑭ I am three less than double one-third of 21.

⑮ I am five more than a fifth of double 20.

⑯ I am half the total of one-sixth of 24 and one-third of 18.

⑰ I am the difference between one-quarter of 60 and one-fifth of 60.

⑱ I am the total of one-half, one-third and one-quarter of 24.

THINK Invent your own 'Who am I?' problems using fractions. Write down the answers secretly and test them on a partner.

○
○ **I am confident with finding non-unit fractions of**
○ **amounts.**

Finding equivalent and simplest fractions

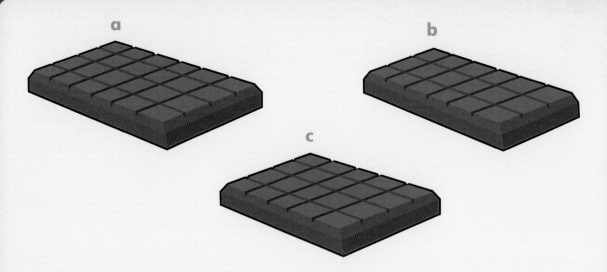

a   b

c

1. Draw chocolate bar 'a' on squared paper and shade $\frac{1}{8}$ of it.

2. How many $\frac{1}{8}$s make $\frac{1}{2}$?

3. Draw chocolate bar 'b' twice. Shade $\frac{1}{6}$ of one bar and $\frac{1}{9}$ of the other.

4. How many $\frac{1}{6}$s make $\frac{1}{3}$?

5. How many $\frac{1}{9}$s make $\frac{1}{3}$?

6. Draw chocolate bar 'c' and shade $\frac{1}{10}$.

7. How many $\frac{1}{10}$s make $\frac{1}{2}$?

8. How many $\frac{1}{10}$s make $\frac{1}{5}$?

THINK   A chocolate bar has 60 squares. You eat half of it. How many different fractions can you write to show the amount you have eaten?

I am confident with finding equivalent fractions.

28

Write three more fractions for each fraction family below.

1. $\frac{1}{2}$ $\frac{2}{4}$ $\frac{3}{6}$ —   —   —

2. $\frac{1}{3}$ $\frac{2}{6}$ $\frac{3}{?}$ —   —   —

3. $\frac{2}{3}$ $\frac{4}{6}$ —   —   —   —

4. $\frac{1}{4}$ …

5. $\frac{3}{4}$ …

6. $\frac{1}{5}$ …

7. $\frac{4}{5}$ …

Write each fraction in its simplest form.

8. $\frac{7}{14}$

9. $\frac{4}{12}$

10. $\frac{5}{20}$

11. $\frac{6}{9}$

12. $\frac{18}{24}$

13. $\frac{30}{40}$

14. $\frac{10}{50}$

15. $\frac{8}{12}$

16. $\frac{7}{28}$

17. $\frac{6}{30}$

18. $\frac{18}{27}$

19. $\frac{16}{24}$

THINK A fraction has a denominator of 36 and its numerator is a 1-digit number between 2 and 10. What could the simplest form of the fraction be? How many possibilities are there?

○ **I am confident with finding equivalent fractions**
○ **and simplifying fractions.**
○

29

Copy this chocolate bar twice.

1 Shade $\frac{9}{12}$ of the first one.
Write $\frac{9}{12}$ in its simplest form.

2 Shade $\frac{8}{12}$ of the second one.
Write $\frac{8}{12}$ in its simplest form.

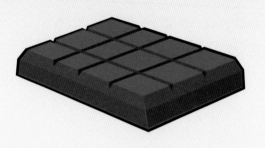

Write each fraction in its simplest form.

3 $\frac{10}{12}$ **6** $\frac{25}{30}$ **9** $\frac{15}{50}$ **12** $\frac{10}{25}$

4 $\frac{8}{24}$ **7** $\frac{3}{24}$ **10** $\frac{15}{18}$ **13** $\frac{27}{36}$

5 $\frac{12}{20}$ **8** $\frac{12}{48}$ **11** $\frac{21}{28}$ **14** $\frac{15}{24}$

15 Write which of these fractions are equivalent to $\frac{3}{8}$.

$\frac{9}{24}$ $\frac{12}{32}$ $\frac{30}{80}$ $\frac{6}{40}$ $\frac{33}{88}$ $\frac{21}{54}$ $\frac{15}{50}$ $\frac{60}{160}$

16 Explain in words how you can recognise fractions that are equivalent to $\frac{3}{8}$.

| 1 | 2 | 3 | 4 | 5 | 6 | 7 | 8 | 9 | 10 |

THINK Use pairs of numbers from the cards above to make fractions that are less than 1. Make four that cannot be simplified and four that can.

○
○ **I am confident with simplifying fractions.**
○

Copy and complete the table to show the types of angle in each polygon.

	Acute	Right angle	Obtuse
1	2	1	0

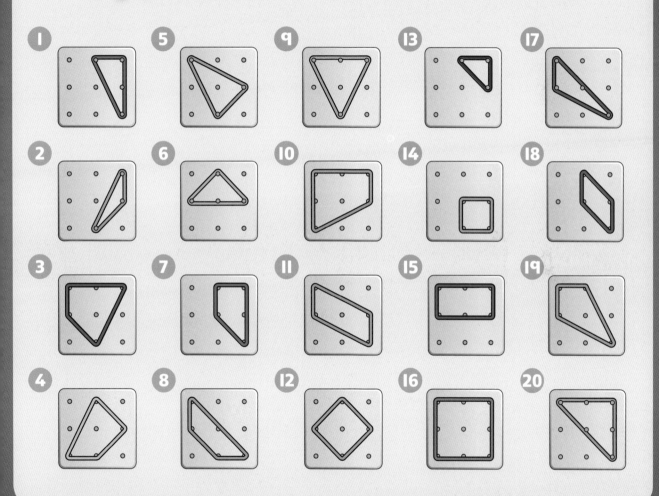

THINK Write your name in capital letters. In which letters can you see an acute angle?

I am confident with identifying acute, right and obtuse angles.

Write whether each angle is acute, right or obtuse.

Write whether each angle given below is acute, right or obtuse.

2 45°	**5** 110°	**8** 90°	**11** 164°
3 30°	**6** 175°	**9** 15°	**12** 33°
4 95°	**7** 11°	**10** 125°	**13** 91°

THINK Can you think of any capital letters that have two or more acute angles? If so write them down.

○
○ **I am confident with identifying acute, right and**
○ **obtuse angles.**

Parallel and perpendicular

For each shape write whether it has any parallel sides. If it does write how many pairs of parallel sides it has.

Then write whether each shape has any perpendicular lines.

THINK Write four capital letters with perpendicular lines and four with parallel lines.

○ **I am confident with identifying parallel and**
○ **perpendicular lines.**
○

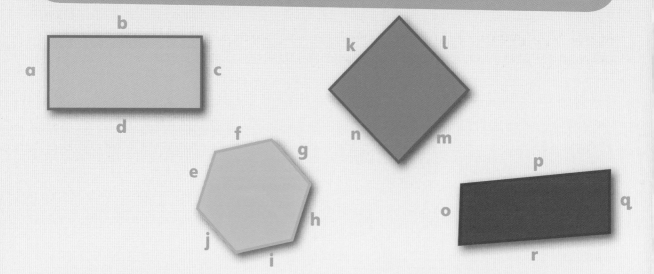

1. parallel to b
2. perpendicular to m
3. parallel to r
4. perpendicular to a
5. parallel to f
6. parallel to c

7. perpendicular to k
8. parallel to h
9. parallel to o
10. parallel to j
11. parallel to d
12. parallel to q

True or false? Discuss with a partner.

13. All rectangles have two pairs of parallel sides.
14. If a square has horizontal sides then it also has vertical sides.
15. A regular hexagon has three pairs of parallel sides.
16. The angle between a horizontal line and a vertical line is a right angle.
17. A regular pentagon has perpendicular sides.
18. An equilateral triangle has perpendicular sides.

I am confident with identifying parallel and perpendicular lines.

Properties of 2D shapes

Read the clues and write down the letter and name of the shape that each set of clues describes.

①

It has 4 equal sides and 4 equal angles.

③

It has only one set of parallel sides.

⑤

It is a regular hexagon.

⑦

It has 7 sides and 7 angles.

②

It has 9 sides. Some are perpendicular and some are parallel.

④

It has only one pair of perpendicular sides.

⑥

It has 2 equal obtuse angles and 2 unequal acute angles.

⑧

It has two pairs of parallel sides but no perpendicular sides.

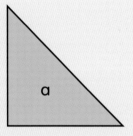

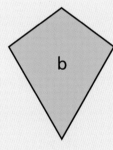

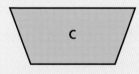

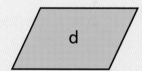

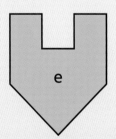

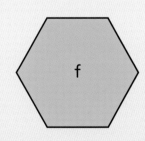

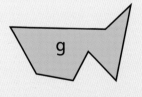

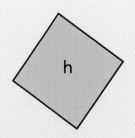

THINK Write your own clues for a shape. Ask a partner to guess the shape.

○
○ **I am confident with identifying shapes by their**
○ **properties.**

Study the pattern below.

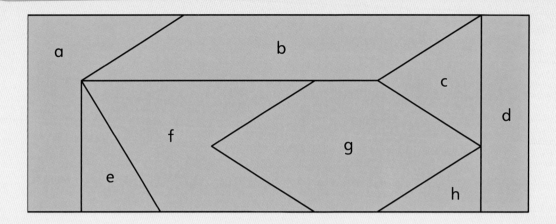

Answer these questions about the shapes in the pattern.

1. How many triangles in the pattern have perpendicular sides?

2. Which quadrilateral has two pairs of parallel sides but no perpendicular ones?

3. How many pairs of parallel sides does shape *a* have?

4. Which shapes have at least one line of symmetry?

5. Which shapes have no right angles?

6. Which shape has only acute angles?

7. Which shapes have at least one pair of parallel sides but no perpendicular ones?

True or false?

8. Shape *a* has 3 right angles and 2 acute angles.

9. Shape *g* is a regular hexagon.

10. Every shape in the pattern has at least one side that is parallel or perpendicular to one of the sides of shape *d*.

I am confident with identifying properties of shapes.

Draw triangles, quadrilaterals, pentagons or hexagons with:

1 two acute angles

2 two obtuse angles

3 two right angles

4 two parallel sides

5 two pairs of perpendicular lines

6 two lines of symmetry

Which of these are possible and which are impossible?

7 Drawing a triangle with two obtuse angles.

8 Drawing a triangle with three lines of symmetry.

9 Drawing a quadrilateral with two obtuse and two acute angles.

10 Drawing a quadrilateral with exactly three right angles.

11 Drawing a pentagon with only two lines of symmetry.

12 Drawing a hexagon with two acute angles.

I am confident with drawing shapes with given properties.

Lines of symmetry

Use a mirror to check Bill's homework.
Which lines of symmetry did he get wrong?

1
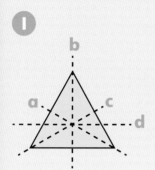

2
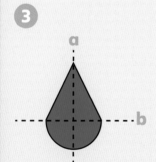

3

4
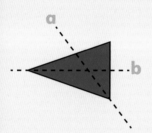

5
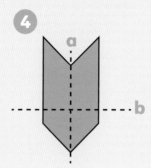

6
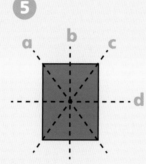

7
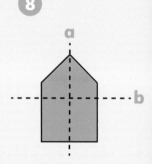

8
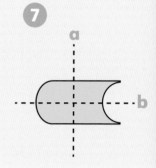

9
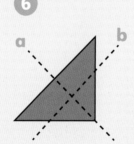

THINK Draw a line of symmetry.
Draw a triangle on either
side of it. Build up a
symmetrical pattern.

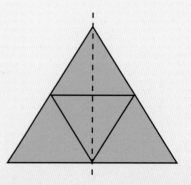

○○○ I am confident with identifying symmetry within
shapes.

38

Copy and complete each shape and its reflection in the dotted mirror line.

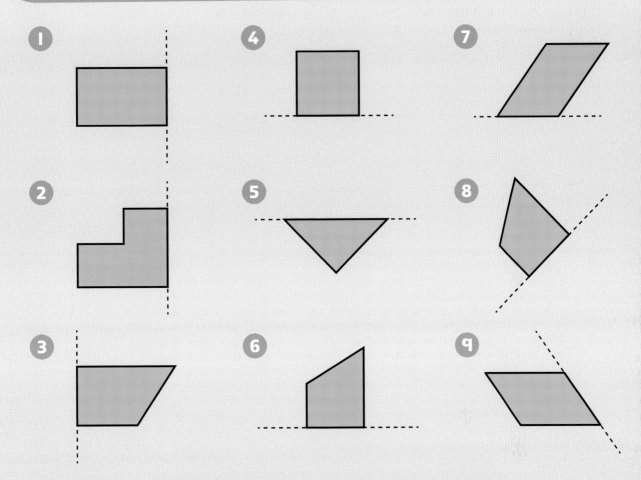

1.

2.

3.

4.

5.

6.

7.

8.

9.

10. Draw a quadrilateral with two lines of symmetry.

11. Draw a pentagon with one line of symmetry.

12. Draw a hexagon with two lines of symmetry.

13. Draw a kite with one line of symmetry.

14. Draw round a regular pentagon and draw in the lines of symmetry.

15. Draw a polygon with four lines of symmetry.

16. Draw a polygon with no lines of symmetry.

○ **I am confident with lines of symmetry within shapes.**
○
○

Dividing 2- and 3-digit numbers by 1-digit numbers

$$10 \times 6 = 60$$
$$20 \times 6 = 120$$
$$30 \times 6 = 180$$

$96 \div 6 = \square$ $96 \div 6 = 16$

$\square \times 6 = 96$
$\underline{10 \times 6 = 60}$
36
$\underline{6 \times 6 = 36}$
0

16

$1 \times 6 = 6$
$2 \times 6 = 12$
$3 \times 6 = 18$
$4 \times 6 = 24$
$5 \times 6 = 30$
$6 \times 6 = 36$

Perform these divisions.

1. $95 \div 5 = \square$
2. $57 \div 3 = \square$
3. $72 \div 4 = \square$
4. $108 \div 6 = \square$
5. $120 \div 5 = \square$
6. $132 \div 6 = \square$

There are 144 children at sports day.

7. How many teams of 3 can be made?
8. How many teams of 4 can be made?
9. How many teams of 6 can be made?

There are 168 cupcakes at a bakery.

10. How many boxes of 4 cupcakes can be made?
11. How many boxes of 6 cupcakes can be made?

There are 114 photos to put in an album.

12. How many pages will be used if there are 3 photos per page?
13. How many pages will be used if there are 6 photos per page?

THINK What number between 50 and 80 can be divided by 2, 3, 4, 5 and 6 without leaving a remainder?

○
○
○ **I am confident with dividing 2- and 3-digit numbers by 3, 4, 5 and 6.**

Perform these divisions.

1 $56 \div 4 = \square$ **6** $126 \div 6 = \square$

2 $72 \div 3 = \square$ **7** $136 \div 8 = \square$

3 $102 \div 6 = \square$ **8** $117 \div 9 = \square$

4 $115 \div 5 = \square$ **9** $138 \div 6 = \square$

5 $112 \div 7 = \square$ **10** $133 \div 7 = \square$

Solve these problems.

11 One sheet of stickers costs 7p. How many sheets can Max buy with 98p?

12 Stickers come in sheets of 8. How many sheets of 8 stickers does Karl have if he has 144 stickers altogether?

13 Karl arranges his 144 stickers into a sticker book. He puts 6 stickers on each page of the book. How many pages does he use?

14 At the vet, Kim is told her dog must take tablets that come in packs of 9. How many packs are there if she is given 117 tablets?

15 Kim's dog must take 3 tablets each day. They have 117 tablets. After how many days will they run out of tablets?

16 Sarah's dog is also ill. She must put 7 ml of medicine into his water bowl each day. She is given 105 ml of medicine. After how many days will they run out?

 **THINK** Make up your own grouping division question for $152 \div 8$.

> I am confident with dividing 2- and 3-digit numbers by 1-digit numbers.

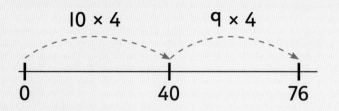

10 × 4   9 × 4

0   40   76

$$10 \times 4 = 40$$
$$20 \times 4 = 80$$
$$30 \times 4 = 120$$

$76 \div 4 = \square$ $76 \div 4 = 19$

$\square \times 4 = 76$
$10 \times 4 = 40$
       36
$9 \times 4 = 36$
        0
19

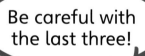

$1 \times 4 = 4$
$2 \times 4 = 8$
$3 \times 4 = 12$
$4 \times 4 = 16$
$5 \times 4 = 20$
$6 \times 4 = 24$
$7 \times 4 = 28$
$8 \times 4 = 32$
$9 \times 4 = 36$

1 $65 \div 5 = \square$ **6** $96 \div 4 = \square$

2 $72 \div 3 = \square$ **7** $84 \div 6 = \square$

3 $92 \div 4 = \square$ **8** $59 \div 3 = \square$

4 $75 \div 5 = \square$ **9** $83 \div 4 = \square$

5 $42 \div 3 = \square$ **10** $67 \div 3 = \square$

Be careful with the last three!

THINK How can you tell, before you start working out your division, whether you will write a 10 or 20 as the first number to multiply by the divisor?

I am confident with dividing 2- and 3-digit numbers by 1-digit numbers with and without remainders.

Before each division, predict whether there will be a remainder or not. Then answer them.

1. $72 \div 4 = \square$

2. $89 \div 5 = \square$

3. $88 \div 3 = \square$

4. $89 \div 6 = \square$

5. $77 \div 4 = \square$

6. $94 \div 8 = \square$

7. $99 \div 4 = \square$

8. $126 \div 6 = \square$

9. $70 \div 3 = \square$

10. $112 \div 8 = \square$

11. $138 \div 6 = \square$

12. $178 \div 8 = \square$

13. $145 \div 6 = \square$

14. $184 \div 8 = \square$

15. $117 \div 5 = \square$

16. $153 \div 6 = \square$

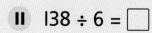

THINK How can you tell, before you start working out your division, whether there will be a remainder or not?

I am confident with dividing 2- and 3-digit numbers by 1-digit numbers, with and without remainders.

Divide these numbers, giving remainders where necessary.

1 142 ÷ 5 = ☐

2 157 ÷ 6 = ☐

3 109 ÷ 4 = ☐

4 161 ÷ 7 = ☐

5 87 ÷ 3 = ☐

6 210 ÷ 8 = ☐

7 243 ÷ 9 = ☐

8 117 ÷ 6 = ☐

9 150 ÷ 8 = ☐

10 168 ÷ 7 = ☐

11 253 ÷ 9 = ☐

12 166 ÷ 6 = ☐

13 178 ÷ 8 = ☐

14 175 ÷ 6 = ☐

15 245 ÷ 8 = ☐

16 262 ÷ 9 = ☐

17 167 ÷ 7 = ☐

18 242 ÷ 9 = ☐

THINK Choose a number between 5 and 10. Which numbers between 60 and 100 give a remainder of 1 when divided by your number?

●
● **I am confident with dividing 2- and 3-digit numbers**
● **by 1-digit numbers, with and without remainders.**

Using factors to multiply and divide

Write all the factor pairs for these numbers.

1 12

2 18

3 20

4 24

5 30

6 36

Factor pairs are pairs of numbers that multiply to give another number!

Use the factor pairs of 20 to answer these multiplications and divisions.

7 50 × 4 = ☐

8 200 ÷ 5 = ☐

9 100 × 2 = ☐

10 200 ÷ 4 = ☐

Write the factor pairs of 28 and use them to answer these multiplications and divisions.

11 40 × 7 = ☐

12 280 ÷ 7 = ☐

13 2 × 140 = ☐

14 280 ÷ 4 = ☐

THINK Write one number that has the factors 2, 3, 4 and 5.

I am confident with identifying factor pairs and using them to answer related multiplications and divisions.

Write all the factor pairs for these numbers.

1 20

2 28

3 42

4 33

5 45

6 48

7 54

Factor pairs are pairs of numbers that multiply to give another number!

Write the factor pairs of 24 and use them to answer these multiplications and divisions.

8 $30 \times 8 = \square$

9 $240 \div 6 = \square$

10 $12 \times 20 = \square$

11 $240 \div 4 = \square$

Write the factor pairs of 36 and use them to answer these multiplications and divisions.

12 $30 \times 12 = \square$

13 $360 \div 6 = \square$

14 $4 \times 90 = \square$

15 $360 \div 9 = \square$

 **THINK** If 4 and 9 are both factors of a number, which numbers less than 100 could it be?

I am confident with identifying factor pairs and using them to answer related multiplications and divisions.

Write all the factor pairs for these numbers.

1 16

2 28

3 39

4 56

5 54

6 60

7 66

8 72

Write the factor pairs of 36 and use them to answer these multiplications and divisions.

9 120 × 3 = ☐

10 360 ÷ 3 = ☐

11 180 × 2 = ☐

12 360 ÷ 6 = ☐

Write the factor pairs of 64 and use them to answer these multiplications and divisions.

13 80 × 4 = ☐

14 640 ÷ 4 = ☐

15 16 × 40 = ☐

16 640 ÷ 8 = ☐

Use known factor pairs to answer these multiplications and divisions.

17 40 × 7 = ☐

18 280 ÷ 7 = ☐

19 2 × 140 = ☐

20 280 ÷ 4 = ☐

 **THINK** Write a number larger than 50 that has 2, 3, 4 and 9 as factors.

I am confident with identifying factor pairs and using them to answer related multiplications and divisions.

Subtract by counting up to multiples of 1000

Complete these subtractions using Frog.

1 1000 − 750 = ☐

2 1000 − 825 = ☐

3 1000 − 915 = ☐

4 1000 − 865 = ☐

5 1000 − 532 = ☐

6 1000 − 478 = ☐

7 1000 − 267 = ☐

8 1000 − 349 = ☐

9 3000 − 2575 = ☐

10 7000 − 6725 = ☐

11 4000 − 3672 = ☐

12 2000 − 1438 = ☐

 **THINK** How many times can you subtract 175 from 1000 without going into negative numbers? The first two subtractions have been done for you below.

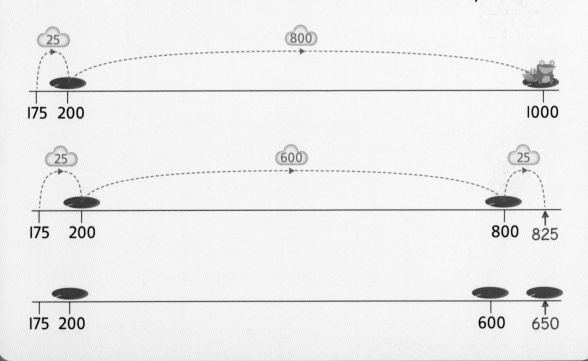

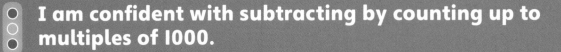

I am confident with subtracting by counting up to multiples of 1000.

Complete these subtractions. Use Frog.

1 1000 − 638 = ☐

2 1000 − 425 = ☐

3 1000 − 344 = ☐

4 1000 − 478 = ☐

5 1000 − 286 = ☐

6 3000 − 2463 = ☐

7 5000 − 4661 = ☐

8 2000 − 1322 = ☐

9 7000 − 6289 = ☐

10 6000 − 5267 = ☐

11 9000 − 8304 = ☐

12 8000 − 7075 = ☐

13 7000 − 5725 = ☐

14 4000 − 2645 = ☐

15 6000 − 3439 = ☐

16 8000 − 5583 = ☐

17 9000 − 5673 = ☐

18 5000 − 1428 = ☐

THINK How many times can you subtract 775 from 10 000 without going into negative numbers?

I am confident with subtracting by counting up to multiples of 1000.

Subtract to find change from £10, £20 or £50

Find change from £10.

① £6·54

② £5·87

③ £4·36

④ £7·43

Find change from £20. Write the notes and coins you could use to give the change.

⑤ £13·08

⑥ £17·24

⑦ £11·79

⑧ £8·72

Solve these problems.

⑨ Mrs Sharma must pay £3·35 in a car park. She puts a £10 note into the machine. How much change should she get?

⑩ Jack has £20. How much change will he get if he buys a magazine costing £3·89?

⑪ How much change from £50 would you get if you bought an mp4 player for £42·65? Which notes and coins might you be given?

THINK If you pay £10 for a cake that costs £☐·☐☐ and the change given is three coins of different values, what could the cake cost?

 I am confident with finding change from £10, £20 and £50, using the method of counting up.

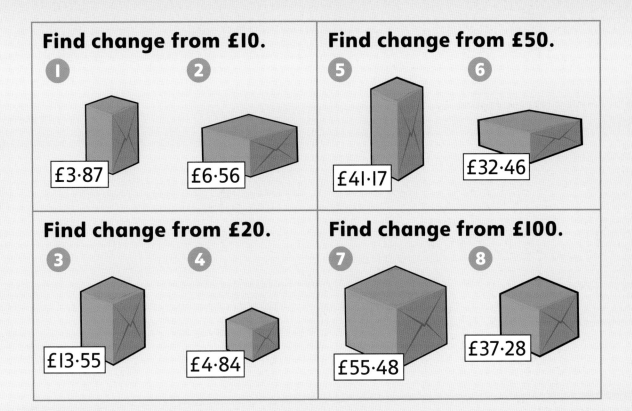

Find change from £10.

① £3·87

② £6·56

Find change from £50.

⑤ £41·17

⑥ £32·46

Find change from £20.

③ £13·55

④ £4·84

Find change from £100.

⑦ £55·48

⑧ £37·28

Solve these problems.

⑨ I spent £10 and bought a T-shirt. I was given £3·51 change. How much did the T-shirt cost?

⑩ Miss Jones was given a £2 coin, a £1 coin and a 20p coin in change from a ticket machine in a car park. She had paid with a £10 note. How much had the ticket cost?

⑪ I spent £20 and bought two magazines of the same price. My change was £8·46. How much did each magazine cost?

⑫ Josef was given £50 for his birthday. He bought three DVDs and now has £26·03 left. If all the DVDs cost the same, how much did each cost?

 If you pay £10 for a torch that costs £☐·☐☐ and the change given is four different coins, what could the torch cost?

○○○ **I am confident with finding change from £10, £20, £50 and £100 using the method of counting up.**

Place value of decimal numbers

Write the decimal number shown by each tag.

1
0   1

2
1   2

3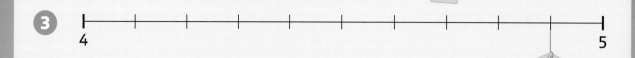
4   5

4
7   8

5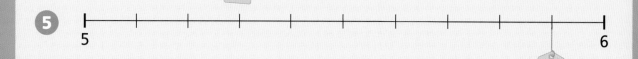
5   6

6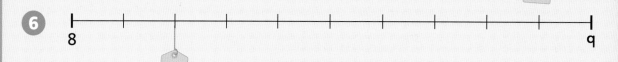
8   q

7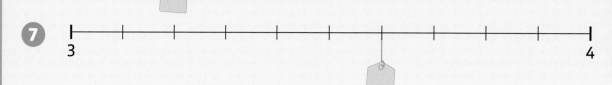
3   4

8 Draw a 0–1 number line. Mark on 0·5.

THINK Draw a 0–1 number line and mark on a decimal number. Ask a partner to work out the number.

○
○ **I am confident with identifying decimal numbers to**
○ **one decimal place on a number line.**

Write the decimal number shown by each tag.

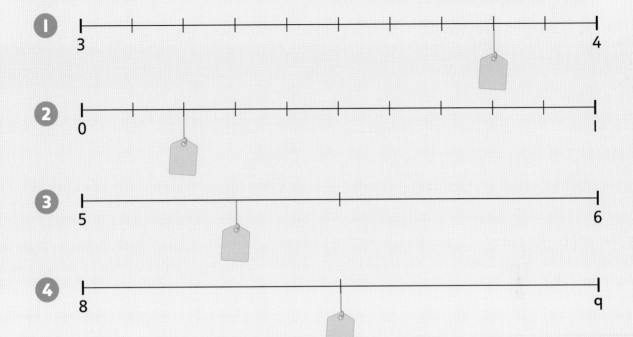

1 3 ——————————————— 4

2 0 ——————————————— 1

3 5 ——————————————— 6

4 8 ——————————————— 9

5 7 ——————————————— 8

6 Draw three number lines of your own. The beginning and end numbers must be one whole number apart. Mark the midpoint on each number line first. Then mark and label three other numbers.

Write the next six numbers in each sequence.

7 0·3, 0·4, 0·5...

8 3·5, 3·6, 3·7...

9 4·7, 4·8, 4·9...

10 9·4, 9·5, 9·6...

THINK Two decimal numbers lie between 2 and 3. They are separated by four tenths on the decimal number line. What could these two numbers be?

I am confident with identifying decimal numbers to one decimal place on a number line, and continuing decimal sequences.

53

Write the decimal numbers for tags a to f.

1

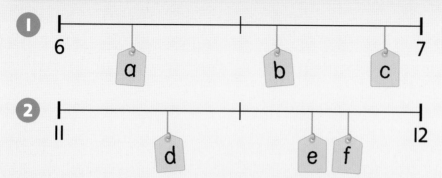

6   a   b   c   7

2

11   d   e   f   12

3 Draw your own number line from 8 to 9 and mark on 8·5, 8·1 and 8·7.

4 Draw your own number line from 7 to 8 and mark on 7·5, 7·2 and 7·9.

Copy the number lines and mark the point given. Write how much to get to the next whole number.

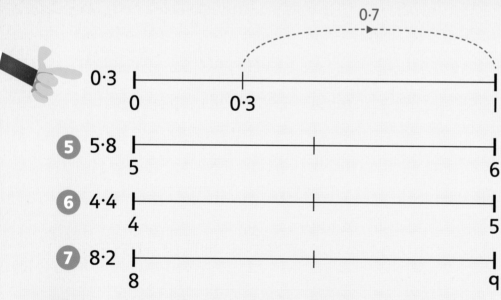

0·7

0·3 | | |
0   0·3   1

5 5·8 | | |
5   6

6 4·4 | | |
4   5

7 8·2 | | |
8   9

THINK How many one place decimal numbers are there between 1·2 and 2·1, between 2·3 and 3·2, and between 3·4 and 4·3? Can you see a pattern?
What are the two middle numbers with one decimal place between 1·2 and 2·1? 2·3 and 3·2? 3·4 and 4·3?

I am confident with identifying a decimal number to one decimal place on a number line and counting to the next whole number.

Draw a < or > sign between each pair of numbers.

1 5·2   4·9

2 3·8   8·3

3 7·6   6·8

4 3·1   2·7

5 9·5   11·2

6 6·5   5·6

7 2·7   2·1

8 8·4   8·8

Round each number to the nearest whole number.

9 2·2

10 2·8

11 8·4

12 7·5

13 9·3

14 3·7

15 5·9

16 4·6

17 Which of these numbers do <u>not</u> round to 7 when rounded to the nearest whole number?

6·6   7·7   7·3   0·7   6·9   6·5   8·7   7·4

 For each of your answers to questions 9 to 16, can you think of another decimal that rounds to the same whole number?

I am confident with comparing decimal numbers to one decimal place and rounding to the next whole number.

55

Draw a < or > sign between each pair of numbers.

1. 3·2   4·2
2. 0·8   8·0
3. 10·2   9·8
4. 7·8   8·7

5. 1·8   11·2
6. 12·5   15·2
7. 0·9   1·1
8. 6·4   4·6

Round each number to the nearest whole number.

9. 8·2
10. 6·6
11. 14·8
12. 11·4

13. 14·2
14. 13·6
15. 9·8
16. 17·5

Solve these problems about children at a diving competition.

17. Cho scored 7·6 for her dive and Anna scored 8·1 for hers. Who had the higher score?

18. Chris's score for a dive was higher than 7·5 and lower than 8·3. What could his score have been, to one decimal place?

5m

19. Write these diving scores in order from smallest to largest:

7·6   7·3   8·0   6·9   5·5   8·7

 How many numbers with one decimal place can you write that round to 3?

I am confident with comparing decimal numbers to one decimal place and rounding to the next whole number.

Divide these numbers by 10.

GRAB! **Place-value grid**

$36 \div 10 = 3{\cdot}6$

100s	10s	1s	0·1s
	3	6	
		3 ·	6

1. $83 \div 10 = \boxed{}$

2. $48 \div 10 = \boxed{}$

3. $77 \div 10 = \boxed{}$

4. $61 \div 10 = \boxed{}$

5. $29 \div 10 = \boxed{}$

6. $52 \div 10 = \boxed{}$

Multiply these numbers by 10.

7. $4{\cdot}7 \times 10 = \boxed{}$

8. $9{\cdot}1 \times 10 = \boxed{}$

9. $3{\cdot}6 \times 10 = \boxed{}$

10. $7{\cdot}8 \times 10 = \boxed{}$

11. $5{\cdot}4 \times 10 = \boxed{}$

12. $8{\cdot}9 \times 10 = \boxed{}$

Divide these numbers by 100.

13. $630 \div 100 = \boxed{}$

14. $780 \div 100 = \boxed{}$

15. $310 \div 100 = \boxed{}$

16. $290 \div 100 = \boxed{}$

17. $650 \div 100 = \boxed{}$

18. $870 \div 100 = \boxed{}$

Multiply these numbers by 100.

19. $3{\cdot}7 \times 100 = \boxed{}$

20. $9{\cdot}1 \times 100 = \boxed{}$

21. $7{\cdot}6 \times 100 = \boxed{}$

22. $4{\cdot}8 \times 100 = \boxed{}$

23. $6{\cdot}4 \times 100 = \boxed{}$

24. $8{\cdot}2 \times 100 = \boxed{}$

 **THINK** Can you think of a 2-digit number that, when divided by 10, does not give a decimal answer?

I am confident with multiplying decimal numbers by 10 and 100, and dividing 2- and 3-digit numbers by 10 and 100.

57

INVESTIGATION

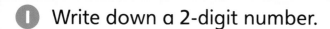

1. Write down a 2-digit number.
2. Divide it by 10.
3. Write down the answer.
4. Repeat steps 1 to 3 seven times.
5. Do you always get a decimal answer?
6. Write a rule for when you will get a decimal answer and when you will not.
7. Follow steps 1 to 3 with the number 30.

Now follow the steps on this scroll.

8. Write down a 3-digit multiple of 10, for example, 420.
9. Divide it by 100.
10. Write down the answer.
11. Repeat steps 1 to 3 seven times.
12. Do you always get a decimal answer?
13. Follow steps 8 to 10 with the number 400.

THINK Write a rule explaining which 3-digit multiples of 10 will give a decimal answer when divided by 100, and which will not.

○
○ **I am confident with multiplying decimal numbers by**
○ **10 and 100, and dividing 2- and 3-digit numbers by 10**
58 and 100.

Adding 4-digit numbers using a written method

GRAB! **Base 10 equipment**

```
   3452        3000   400   50   2
 + 4219      + 4000   200   10   9
    1                       10
 ─────       ──────────────────────
   7671        7000   600   70   1   = 7671
```

THINK Look at questions 1 to 8. In which of them will you need to move a 10 across? A 100 across? A 1000 across?

1
```
   2645        2000   600   40   5
 + 4137      + 4000   100   30   7
 ─────       ──────────────────────
```

2
```
   8352        8000   300   50   2
 + 1384      + 1000   300   80   4
 ─────       ──────────────────────
```

3
```
   1826
 + 4721
 ─────
```

5
```
   7437
 + 1703
 ─────
```

7
```
   3653
 + 4268
 ─────
```

4
```
   2575
 + 3474
 ─────
```

6
```
   4618
 + 4449
 ─────
```

8
```
   5415
 + 7276
 ─────
```

○
○ **I am confident with column addition of two 4-digit**
○ **numbers using the expanded method.**

59

Perform these additions.

$$
\begin{array}{r}
5664 \\
+\ 2737 \\
\hline
\end{array}
\qquad
\begin{array}{r}
5664 \\
+\ 2737 \\
1\ 1\ 1 \\
\hline
8401 \\
\end{array}
$$

1
$$
\begin{array}{r}
8826 \\
+\ 4747 \\
\hline
\end{array}
$$

4
$$
\begin{array}{r}
9676 \\
+\ 6678 \\
\hline
\end{array}
$$

7
$$
\begin{array}{r}
5653 \\
+\ 4768 \\
\hline
\end{array}
$$

2
$$
\begin{array}{r}
6494 \\
+\ 7478 \\
\hline
\end{array}
$$

5
$$
\begin{array}{r}
3756 \\
+\ 8449 \\
\hline
\end{array}
$$

8
$$
\begin{array}{r}
7846 \\
+\ 7279 \\
\hline
\end{array}
$$

3
$$
\begin{array}{r}
5975 \\
+\ 7389 \\
\hline
\end{array}
$$

6
$$
\begin{array}{r}
7668 \\
+\ 4469 \\
\hline
\end{array}
$$

9
$$
\begin{array}{r}
5875 \\
+\ 7276 \\
\hline
\end{array}
$$

Solve these problems.

10 There were 7183 men and 3785 women at a rugby match. How many altogether?

11 Min ran 7254 m on Monday and 4748 m on Wednesday. How far is this altogether?

What must 'S' be?

THINK

$$
\begin{array}{r}
S\ N\ O\ W \\
+\ R\ A\ I\ N \\
\hline
S\ L\ E\ E\ T \\
\end{array}
$$

Each letter is a different digit number. Can you find what number each letter represents to make this addition work?

I am confident with column addition of two 4-digit numbers using the compact method.

Solve these problems.

1 At a music website, 7483 people downloaded the album *Fire* on Saturday and 3785 downloaded it on Sunday. How many downloads is this altogether?

2 Another album called *17* was downloaded by 6879 people on Saturday and 4675 on Sunday. How many downloads is this altogether?

3 A new track only sold 2563 on its first day on sale. On its second day it was played on the radio and then sold 6785 more than on the first day. How many were sold in total on both days?

4 In a weekly TV talent show there are four contestants left. This week Kai got 1047 votes, Josie got 4782 votes, and Gigi got 3817 more votes than Josie. Kacey was the winner with 3136 more votes than Gigi. How many votes did Kacey get?

5 The next week Gigi got 5356 votes, Josie got 1247 more than Gigi, and Kacey got 6647 votes. Who got more – Josie or Kacey – and by how many more did they win?

6 In the final week Josie got 6864 votes and Kacey got 6983 votes. How many more than 10 000 people voted in total?

 **THINK** Write your own 2-step word problem for a partner to solve.

○
○ **I am confident with column addition of two 4-digit**
○ **numbers.**

61

Adding amounts of money

Use a mental method for these additions.

1 £21 + £44 = ☐

2 £35 + £35 + £20 = ☐

3 £22 + £11 + £44 = ☐

4 £25 + £25 + £16 = ☐

5 £26 + £32 + £24 = ☐

6 £99 + £32 = ☐

7 £66 + £33 + £5 = ☐

8 £25 + £75 + £69 = ☐

9 £33 + £18 + £47 = ☐

10 £345 + £102 = ☐

11 £465 + £199 = ☐

12 £548 + £221 = ☐

Use a written method for these additions.

13 £37 + £17 + £48 = ☐

14 £56 + £27 + £75 = ☐

15 £76 + £68 + £78 = ☐

16 £55 + £87 + £79 = ☐

17 £66 + £78 + £47 = ☐

18 £527 + £147 = ☐

19 £378 + £576 = ☐

20 £678 + £537 = ☐

Remember to set them out in columns and add the 1s first.

 THINK Write an addition of three 2-digit numbers where the total of the 1s digits is exactly 10.

○ **I am confident with adding 2- and 3-digit numbers using mental and written methods.**

Perform these additions using either a mental or written method.

1. £27 + £73 + £42 = ☐
2. £67 + £44 + £58 = ☐
3. £35 + £60 + £45 = ☐
4. £42 + £81 + £57 = ☐
5. £78 + £73 + £65 = ☐
6. £45 + £87 + £45 = ☐
7. £24 + £28 + £98 = ☐
8. £44 + £87 + £77 = ☐
9. £66 + £84 + £33 = ☐
10. £83 + £76 + £69 = ☐
11. £247 + £802 = ☐
12. £567 + £274 = ☐
13. £634 + £798 = ☐
14. £755 + £688 = ☐
15. £467 + £521 = ☐
16. £648 + £537 = ☐

Solve these problems using either a mental or written method.

17. Jay has two bank accounts. In one he has £375 and in the other he has £723. How much has he altogether?

18. Ed buys three items of clothing from a shop. The items cost £28, £34 and £37. How much change from £100 does she get?

19. Mrs Collins buys a laptop costing £779 and a printer costing £387. She is then given a £10 discount for buying them together. How much does she pay?

 **THINK** Write an addition of three 2-digit numbers where the total is exactly 100. The 1s digits must not be 0 or 5.

I am confident with adding 2- and 3-digit numbers using mental and written methods.

Perform these additions using either a mental or written method.

1. £87 + £43 + £45 = ☐
2. £79 + £44 + £56 = ☐
3. £47 + £68 + £85 = ☐
4. £53 + £71 + £56 = ☐
5. £85 + £66 + £78 = ☐
6. £48 + £37 + £86 = ☐
7. £52 + £78 + £98 = ☐
8. £54 + £45 + £77 = ☐
9. £247 + £878 = ☐
10. £698 + £443 = ☐
11. £647 + £332 = ☐
12. £825 + £274 = ☐
13. £877 + £768 = ☐
14. £358 + £688 = ☐
15. £469 + £231 = ☐
16. £956 + £548 = ☐

Solve these problems using either a mental or written method.

17. Two TVs are for sale. One costs £467 more than the other. If the cheaper TV costs £278, what does the more expensive one cost?

18. Three brothers decide to raise money for charity by doing odd-jobs. Ben raises £28, Rob raises £46 and Max raises £37. How much more than £100 do they raise in total?

19. Jude is training for the Olympics and buys a bike costing £379. The special helmet he needs costs £123. How much more than £500 does he need to buy both?

 **THINK** Write three 3-digit + 3-digit additions that you would solve using a mental method. Then write three that you would solve using a written method.

Subtracting amounts of money

Choose whether to count up using Frog or take away for each subtraction.

1 £56·80 – £10·10 = ☐

2 £60 – £47·86 = ☐

3 £7·94 – £0·48 = ☐

4 £35·80 – £4·30 = ☐

5 £40·50 – £38·75 = ☐

6 £22 – £2·50 = ☐

7 £22 – £19·95 = ☐

8 £100 – £73·98 = ☐

9 £47·73 – £20·50 = ☐

10 £28·80 – £7·20 = ☐

11 £43·12 – £42·86 = ☐

12 £45·76 – £40 = ☐

Are these statements true or false?

13 If the larger number in a subtraction has two zeros, it is easier to use Frog than column subtraction.

14 If you are working out change, you should always use Frog.

15 If the number being subtracted is really small, it is best to take away or count back.

 **THINK** Write three subtraction questions. Write one that you think is best solved by using Frog, one by counting back, and one by using place value.

I am confident with choosing a mental method to subtract amounts of money.

Solve the problems below, choosing whether to count up using Frog or take away for each subtraction.

£44·38   £64·95   £37·89   £27·48   £52·74   £29·44

You have £50. How much change will you get if you buy:

1. a game for £37·89?
2. a skateboard for £29·44?
3. a doll's house for £27·48?
4. a train set for £44·38?

5. The construction kit is being reduced in price. It cost £52·74. What will it cost after being reduced by £3·50?

6. Kat wants to buy a scooter costing £64·95, but has only saved £62·60. How much more money does she need?

7. At a buy-and-sell fair, you sell a computer console for £45·90. You then buy an electronic robot for £30·63. How much money do you have left?

8. Sunil's mum gives him £32 towards buying the £44·38 train set. How much money does Sunil need to pay himself?

Are these statements true or false?

9. It is easiest to subtract from a multiple of 100 by counting up.
10. It is easiest to take away if it is an exact number of pounds being subtracted.

○
○ **I am confident with choosing a mental method**
○ **to subtract amounts of money.**

Subtract using a written method

 GRAB! **Base 10 equipment**

£425 – £242 = £183

```
    3 12
  4 2 5
-  2 4 2
  1 8 3
```

Use compact column subtraction to perform these.

1 £573 – £334 = ☐

2 £684 – £291 = ☐

3 £578 – £359 = ☐

4 £975 – £684 = ☐

5 £558 – £385 = ☐

6 £967 – £375 = ☐

7 £674 – £538 = ☐

8 £759 – £482 = ☐

9 £539 – £242 = ☐

10 £825 – £634 = ☐

Solve these problems.

11 Simon has saved £812. Amit has saved £561. How much more must Amit save to have as much as Simon?

12 Hannah has £349 in her bank account. She buys a bicycle for £284. How much does she have left?

13 Lee receives a bill for £629. He has £478. How much more does he need to pay the bill?

 **THINK** Write a word problem for a partner to solve where they need to do a column subtraction.

○
○ **I am confident with subtracting amounts of money**
○ **using compact column subtraction.**

Perform these using a written method.

1 673 – 456 = ☐   **3** 428 – 265 = ☐

2 483 – 267 = ☐   **4** 857 – 762 = ☐

Perform these using Frog to count up.

5 807 – 764 = ☐   **7** 410 – 367 = ☐

6 702 – 683 = ☐   **8** 908 – 859 = ☐

Answer these using place-value subtraction or by taking away (counting back).

9 526 – 302 = ☐   **11** 578 – 312 = ☐

10 689 – 201 = ☐   **12** 867 – 605 = ☐

Choose an appropriate method to answer these subtractions.

13 795 – 311 = ☐   **15** 759 – 204 = ☐

14 567 – 472 = ☐   **16** 803 – 767 = ☐

 **THINK** Look at the numbers in the subtractions on this page and say what you notice about Frog numbers and what you notice about column subtraction numbers.

Look at the 10s and 1s digits.

○○○ I am confident with subtraction using a variety of mental and written methods.

Choose to use Frog, column or taking away for each subtraction.

1 £502 − £468 = ☐

2 £640 − £576 = ☐

3 £873 − £348 = ☐

4 £707 − £684 = ☐

5 £729 − £184 = ☐

6 £410 − £358 = ☐

7 £478 − £213 = ☐

8 £862 − £359 = ☐

Solve these problems.

9 Jane has saved £228. She spends £156 on a holiday. How much does she have left?

10 A laptop is reduced in price from £450 to £387. By how much is it reduced?

11 Etti has £846 in a bank account. Jade has £538 less than Etti. How much does Jade have?

12 Kip wants to buy a bike that costs £409. So far he has saved £278. How much more does he need to save?

13 Dean has a bill to pay that is £320. He has £478. How much will he have left once he has paid the bill?

14 Sara's bill is £367. At the moment she only has £286. How much more does she need to pay the bill?

THINK Write a 3-digit − 2-digit subtraction that gives an answer of £89. Can you write another that gives the same answer? And another?

I am confident with subtraction using a variety of mental and written methods.

Choose a suitable method for each subtraction.

1. 602 – 487 = ☐

2. 464 – 281 = ☐

3. 762 – 348 = ☐

4. 808 – 684 = ☐

5. 710 – 348 = ☐

6. 903 – 684 = ☐

7. 618 – 184 = ☐

8. 500 – 318 = ☐

9. 469 – 294 = ☐

10. 578 – 114 = ☐

11. 934 – 274 = ☐

12. 681 – 359 = ☐

Investigate 3-digit subtractions where the answer has a 9 as the Is digit.

☐☐☐ – ☐☐☐ = ☐☐9

or

☐☐☐ – ☐☐☐ = ☐9

13. Find as many examples as you can and look for patterns in the Is digits. Can you explain the patterns?

 **THINK** Find three pairs of numbers with a difference of 685.

○
○ **I am confident with subtraction using a variety of**
○ **mental and written methods.**

24-hour clock

Write these afternoon and evening times as analogue times in words.

1 `16:15`

3 `21:20`

5 `23:10`

7  `19:45`

2 `18:15`

4 `13:25`

6 `14:20`

8 `20:45`

The clocks below all show pm times. Write them as digital 24-hour times.

9

11

13

15

10

12

14

16

THINK What is the largest hour time you use in 24-hour digital times? What is the smallest?

○
○ **I am confident with reading and writing time on a**
○ **24-hour clock.**

Write these afternoon and evening times as analogue times in words.

1. 16:20
3. 21:25
5. 23:55
7. 19:05

2. 18:10
4. 13:40
6. 14:20
8. 20:50

The clocks below all show pm times. Write them as digital 24-hour times.

9. 11. 13. 15.

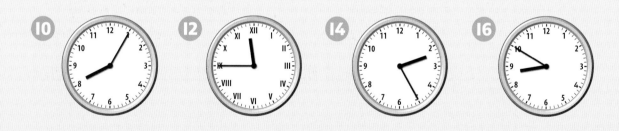

10. 12. 14. 16.

THINK Are there the same number of 'am' times as there are 'pm' times in a day?

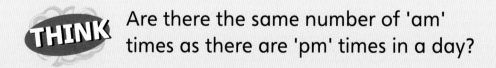

○ **I am confident with reading and writing time on**
○ **a 24-hour clock.**
○

A film starts at 09:45 and finishes at 11:15. How long is the film?

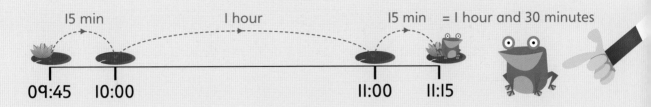

| 15 min | 1 hour | 15 min | = 1 hour and 30 minutes |

09:45   10:00   11:00   11:15

1 A cartoon starts at 11:10 and finishes at 11:45. How long is the cartoon?

2 Sam leaves her house at 08:05 and walks to school. She reaches school at 08:40. For how long does she walk?

3 Jo catches the 07:45 train from London to York. She gets off the train at 09:30. For how long is she on the train?

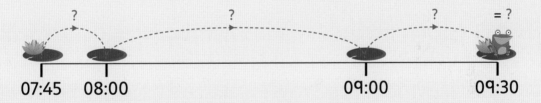

| ? | ? | ? | = ? |

07:45   08:00   09:00   09:30

4 At Amy's school, after assembly finishes at 09:20, classes run until 11:15. For how long do those classes run?

5 Azizi catches the 16:50 train from Leeds to Scarborough. He gets off the train at 18:10. For how long is he on the train?

6 A film starts at 21:20 and finishes at 23:10. How long does it last?

7 Kamna's mum went shopping at 11:30 and finished shopping at 13:05. For how long was she shopping?

8 Fred went for a run. He started at 17:50 and finished at 19:35. How long was his run?

I am confident with working out time intervals by counting up.

Solve these time problems.

Some sausages are put in the oven at 07:53 and are taken out at thirteen minutes past 9. For how long are they in the oven?

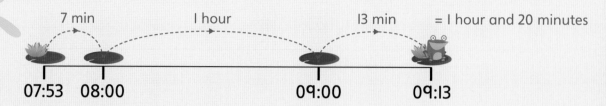

7 min   1 hour   13 min   = 1 hour and 20 minutes

07:53   08:00   09:00   09:13

1. Rosewell School's Sports Day started at 13:35 and finished at quarter past 3. How long did it last?

2. Mrs Smith put a cake in the oven at 10:17. She took it out at two minutes past 12. For how long was it in the oven?

3. Jamie went late-night shopping at quarter to 6 and finished shopping at 19:13. For how long was she shopping?

4. Zoe catches the 16:43 train from Reading to Cardiff. She leaves the train at 18:04. For how long is she on the train?

5. Sara watched a DVD from 19:10 to quarter to 9. For how long did she watch the DVD?

6. Mr Patel leaves his house at 08:09 and drives to work. He reaches there at 09:53. How long is the drive?

7. Julie went jogging. She started at 13:23 and finished at eight minutes to 3. For how long did she jog?

8. A plane takes off at 11:53 and lands at nine minutes to 2. How long is the flight?

THINK Write your own problem, like these, that gives the answer 1 hour and 18 minutes.

○○○ **I am confident with working out time intervals**
by counting up.

Perimeter of rectilinear shapes

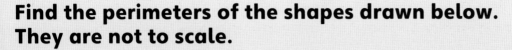

**Find the perimeters of the shapes drawn below.
They are not to scale.**

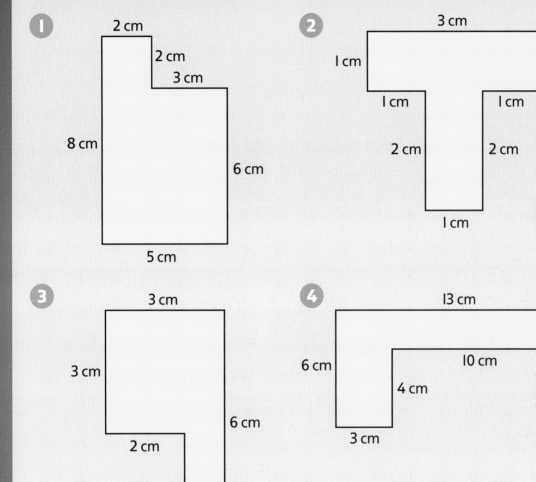

1

2 cm

2 cm

3 cm

8 cm

6 cm

5 cm

2

3 cm

1 cm

1 cm

1 cm

1 cm

2 cm

2 cm

1 cm

3

3 cm

3 cm

2 cm

6 cm

3 cm

1 cm

4

13 cm

2 cm

6 cm

10 cm

4 cm

3 cm

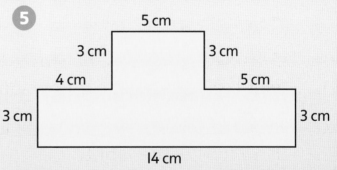

5

5 cm

3 cm

3 cm

4 cm

5 cm

3 cm

3 cm

14 cm

THINK Draw a plan of an L-shaped room that has a perimeter
of 26 m. Mark the lengths of each wall.

○
○ **I am confident with calculating the perimeter of**
○ **shapes made from joined rectangles.**

Find the perimeters of these shapes. They are not to scale.

> You will need to work out the missing lengths.

1
4 cm
2 cm
4 cm

2
3 cm
7 cm
3 cm

3
6 cm
2 cm   2 cm

4
7 cm
5 cm

5
8 cm
8 cm

6
10 cm
5 cm

7
2 cm
2 cm
4 cm
5 cm
3 cm
6 cm

8
4 cm
2 cm
6 cm
5 cm
3 cm
10 cm

 THINK Write a list of the perimeters of squares with sides that are a whole number of centimetres. What do you notice?

○
○ **I am confident with calculating the perimeter of**
○ **rectangles and shapes made from joined rectangles.**

These shapes are not to scale.
Find the perimeters.

You will need to work out the missing lengths.

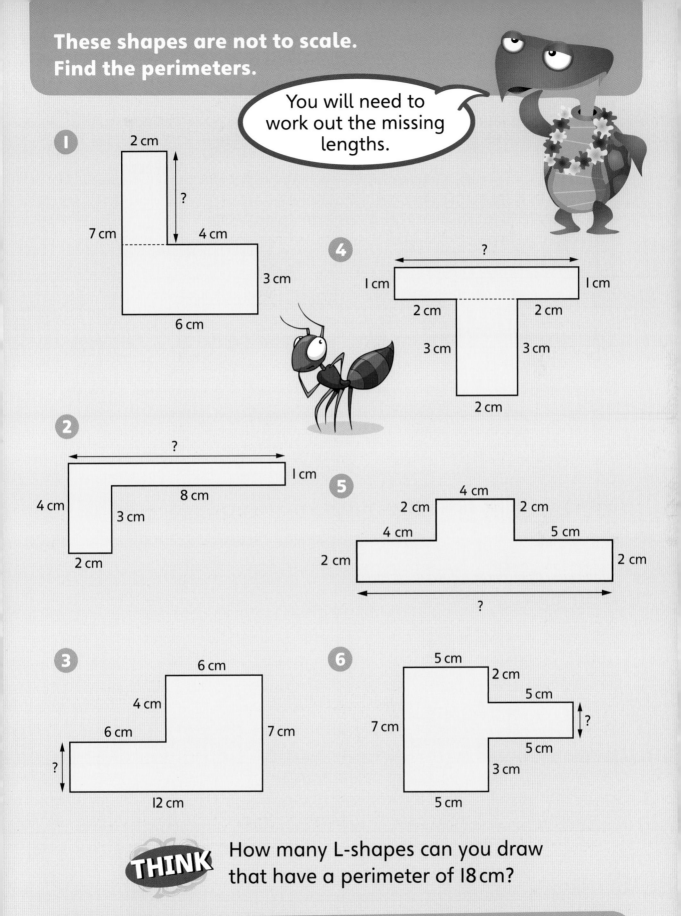

1

2 cm
?
7 cm   4 cm
3 cm
6 cm

4

?
1 cm   1 cm
2 cm   2 cm
3 cm   3 cm
2 cm

2

?
1 cm
8 cm
4 cm
3 cm
2 cm

5

4 cm
2 cm   2 cm
4 cm   5 cm
2 cm   2 cm
?

3

6 cm
4 cm
6 cm   7 cm
?
12 cm

6

5 cm
2 cm
5 cm
7 cm   ?
5 cm
3 cm
5 cm

THINK How many L-shapes can you draw that have a perimeter of 18 cm?

I am confident with calculating missing lengths and the perimeter of shapes made from joined rectangles.

Place Value of 4-digit numbers

Write a number with:

1 three 100s, four 1s, five 10s and six 1000s.

2 six 10s, five 100s, four 1000s and eight 1s.

3 nine 1000s, three 1s, two 10s and one 100.

4 eight 1s, nine 100s, one 1000 and seven 10s.

5 one 100, eight 10s, three 1000s and two 1s.

6 five 10s, nine 1000s, four 1s and three 100s.

Draw a place-value grid and write these numbers on it.

7 four thousand, seven hundred and fifteen.

8 nine thousand, two hundred and twenty-four.

9 seven thousand, three hundred and eleven.

10 six thousand and forty-nine.

Copy and complete.

11 9214 = 8000 + 1200 + ☐

12 6825 = 5000 + ☐ + 25

13 5674 = ☐ + 1600 + 74

 **THINK** A mystery 4-digit number can be partitioned into ☐ 000 + 1500 + ☐ 4. If the mystery number is palindromic (reads the same backwards as forwards) what digits go in the boxes?

○
○ **I am confident with place value of 4-digit numbers.**
○

column subtraction of 4-digit numbers

GRAB! **Base 10 equipment**

2333 – 1215 =

	2000	300	20̶3̶0̶	1̶3̶3̶
–	1000	200	10	5
	1000	100	10	8	= 1118

Use the expanded method for these subtractions.

1

	5000	200	80	2
–	2000	100	30	7

6

	8000	400	60	3
–	3000	200	80	1

2

	6000	800	50	4
–	4000	600	30	6

7

	5000	700	40	7
–	2000	300	50	4

3

	9000	600	50	5
–	2000	300	30	8

8

	6000	700	80	4
–	5000	500	90	2

4

	7000	400	80	1
–	2000	300	70	9

9 6653 – 2732 = ☐

10 3467 – 1732 = ☐

11 4765 – 2935 = ☐

5

	4000	700	80	4
–	2000	600	90	2

12 7537 – 5716 = ☐

THINK

8265 – 7519
Where will you have to move digits? How do you know?

○○○ **I am confident with column subtraction of 4-digit numbers using the expanded method.**

GRAB! Base 10 equipment

$4142 - 1824 =$

	3000	1100	30	12
	~~4000~~	~~100~~	~~40~~	~~2~~
−	1000	800	20	4
	2000	300	10	8	= 2318

1
	5000	200	70	4
−	2000	500	30	7

6
	8000	400	60	3
−	7000	800	80	1

2
	7000	300	70	4
−	4000	600	30	9

7
	5000	700	20	1
−	2000	300	50	4

3
	9000	400	80	5
−	8000	700	30	8

8
	6000	700	30	4
−	4000	800	90	2

4
	7000	200	40	8
−	2000	700	90	4

9 $6253 - 2727 = \square$

10 $3467 - 1739 = \square$

11 $4765 - 3972 = \square$

5
	4000	400	40	4
−	2000	600	90	2

12 $7537 - 5782 = \square$

THINK What digits could go in the boxes below?

3		4	6	−	1		7		=	1	4	7	3

○
○ I am confident with column subtraction of 4-digit
○ numbers using the expanded method.

GRAB! Base 10 equipment

Remember to lay out each subtraction vertically.

	7000	1600		
8636 – 6724 =	~~8000~~	~~600~~	30	6
–	6000	700	20	4
	1000	900	10	2	= 1912

1 7281 – 2239 = ☐

6 7247 – 6324 = ☐

2 8354 – 4632 = ☐

7 8754 – 6591 = ☐

3 7635 – 6293 = ☐

8 6653 – 2439 = ☐

4 8483 – 7872 = ☐

9 8487 – 1738 = ☐

5 6724 – 2393 = ☐

10 7465 – 2937 = ☐

THINK Choose one of the subtractions to check using Frog. Did you get it right? Which method for subtraction do you find easier – the column method or Frog? Which do you usually get a right answer with?

I am confident with column subtraction of 4-digit numbers using the expanded method.

```
                    3000  1200  110   16              3  12 11  16
      4326          4000   300   20    6              4  3  2   6
    − 2847        − 2000   800   40    7          −   2  8  4   7
                    1000   400   70    9              1  4  7   9
```

① 5427
− 2618
_____

⑤ 8569
− 7754
_____

⑨ 9253
− 6794
_____

② 8645
− 2487
_____

⑥ 8452
− 6967
_____

⑩ 8043
− 5867
_____

③ 7364
− 4628
_____

⑦ 3762
− 2975
_____

④ 9832
− 3379
_____

⑧ 4158
− 3775
_____

⑪ Tom scored 4742 points playing a computer game and Anna scored 2586. How many more points did Tom score?

⑫ Gina had £4563 in her bank account. She bought a car costing £1844. How much does she have left in the account now?

 Calculate 6075 − 1824 in two ways: using Frog, then column subtraction. Which method is easier? Write the reason why you think this is.

$$\begin{array}{r} 5133 \\ -\ 4865 \\ \hline \end{array} \qquad \begin{array}{r} {}^{4}\cancel{5}\ {}^{10}\cancel{1}\ {}^{12}\cancel{3}\ {}^{13}\cancel{3} \\ -\ 4\ 8\ 6\ 5 \\ \hline 2\ 6\ 8 \end{array}$$

1
$$\begin{array}{r} 7356 \\ -\ 2848 \\ \hline \end{array}$$

2
$$\begin{array}{r} 8246 \\ -\ 4738 \\ \hline \end{array}$$

3
$$\begin{array}{r} 7124 \\ -\ 4973 \\ \hline \end{array}$$

4
$$\begin{array}{r} 9082 \\ -\ 3676 \\ \hline \end{array}$$

5
$$\begin{array}{r} 8339 \\ -\ 6754 \\ \hline \end{array}$$

6
$$\begin{array}{r} 9532 \\ -\ 3729 \\ \hline \end{array}$$

7
$$\begin{array}{r} 8467 \\ -\ 7683 \\ \hline \end{array}$$

8
$$\begin{array}{r} 8342 \\ -\ 5967 \\ \hline \end{array}$$

9
$$\begin{array}{r} 7834 \\ -\ 2975 \\ \hline \end{array}$$

10
$$\begin{array}{r} 5143 \\ -\ 2855 \\ \hline \end{array}$$

11
$$\begin{array}{r} 7253 \\ -\ 6476 \\ \hline \end{array}$$

12
$$\begin{array}{r} 4122 \\ -\ 3864 \\ \hline \end{array}$$

13
$$\begin{array}{r} 8253 \\ -\ 5757 \\ \hline \end{array}$$

14
$$\begin{array}{r} 7123 \\ -\ 6364 \\ \hline \end{array}$$

THINK What digits could go in the boxes below?

3 [ ] 4 [ ] − 1 [ ] 7 [ ] = 1 4 7 5

I am confident with column subtraction of 4-digit numbers using the compact method.

Choosing a method of subtraction

Answer these subtractions using place value.

1 2549 – 203 = ☐   **3** 8265 – 2014 = ☐

2 8136 – 6002 = ☐   **4** 4626 – 3613 = ☐

Work out these subtractions by counting back.

5 7206 – 120 = ☐   **7** 3745 – 38 = ☐

6 5275 – 52 = ☐   **8** 6210 – 185 = ☐

Answer these subtractions by counting up.

9 9003 – 8975 = ☐   **11** 4040 – 3898 = ☐

10 8005 – 7890 = ☐   **12** 5207 – 4954 = ☐

> Use Frog for counting up.

Perform these subtractions using the column method.

13 4795 – 1587 = ☐   **15** 5666 – 1473 = ☐

14 5479 – 3928 = ☐   **16** 8528 – 3487 = ☐

Choose a method to answer these ones.

17 6362 – 127 = ☐   **19** 8353 – 4862 = ☐

18 6003 – 4981 = ☐   **20** 7837 – 1612 = ☐

THINK How do you know which way to do the last four questions? What is it about the numbers that helps you choose? Discuss with a partner.

I am confident with choosing a method of subtraction.

Choose the best way to perform each subtraction.

1 2549 – 304 = ☐

2 8136 – 5999 = ☐

You could use Frog, place value, column subtraction, rounding or taking away.

3 8265 – 3447 = ☐

4 7006 – 6897 = ☐

5 5275 – 43 = ☐

6 8004 – 7589 = ☐   11 6010 – 5887 = ☐

7 9763 – 2846 = ☐   12 4369 – 206 = ☐

8 4673 – 1030 = ☐   13 5719 – 2436 = ☐

9 4785 – 174 = ☐   14 5666 – 117 = ☐

10 5425 – 4998 = ☐   15 8224 – 3447 = ☐

THINK Write a subtraction, where the answer is 99, which it would be sensible to do using Frog. Now write one with the same answer that it would be sensible to do using place value. Finally, write one with the same answer that would be done using column subtraction.

○
○ **I am confident with choosing a method of**
○ **subtraction.**

85

Multiplying 3-digit numbers by 1-digit numbers

Work through the steps below.

1 Think of a 3-digit number with consecutive digits, e.g. 234.

2 Multiply the number by 9.

3 Write the answer.

4 Do steps 1 to 3 six times.

5 What do you notice about the answers?

6 Think of one more 3-digit number and predict the answer.

7 Now try the same using numbers with descending consecutive digits, e.g. 543.

8 What do you notice about the answers?

THINK Choose different 3-digit numbers that have three identical digits. Multiply each by 9 and describe what you notice about the answers.

 **I am confident with multiplying 3-digit numbers by 9.**

Dividing 2- and 3-digit numbers by 1-digit numbers

Calculate:

1 10 × 5	**3** 30 × 5	**5** 50 × 5
2 20 × 5	**4** 40 × 5	

Use the answers above to work out these divisions.

6 80 ÷ 5	**8** 110 ÷ 5	**10** 115 ÷ 5	**12** 145 ÷ 5
7 95 ÷ 5	**9** 135 ÷ 5	**11** 170 ÷ 5	**13** 220 ÷ 5

Calculate:

14 10 × 7	**16** 30 × 7	**18** 50 × 7
15 20 × 7	**17** 40 × 7	

Use the answers above to work out these divisions.

19 91 ÷ 7	**21** 154 ÷ 7	**23** 217 ÷ 7	**25** 189 ÷ 7
20 147 ÷ 7	**22** 196 ÷ 7	**24** 245 ÷ 7	**26** 301 ÷ 7

Calculate:

27 10 × 6	**29** 30 × 6	**31** 50 × 6
28 20 × 6	**30** 40 × 6	

Use the answers above to work out these divisions.

32 96 ÷ 6	**34** 162 ÷ 6	**36** 174 ÷ 6	**38** 252 ÷ 6
33 150 ÷ 6	**35** 198 ÷ 6	**37** 228 ÷ 6	**39** 204 ÷ 6

 THINK Divide 351 by 9. Then divide 351 by 3. Compare the answers.

○
○ **I am confident with dividing 2- and 3-digit numbers**
○ **by 1-digit numbers.**

Copy and complete these multiplications of 3. Keep going up to 100 × 3.

1 10 × 3   2 20 × 3   3 30 × 3 ...

Use the answers above to work out these divisions.

4 126 ÷ 3   6 114 ÷ 3   8 201 ÷ 3   10 255 ÷ 3

5 162 ÷ 3   7 189 ÷ 3   9 234 ÷ 3   11 288 ÷ 3

Copy and complete these multiplications of 7. Keep going up to 100 × 7.

12 10 × 7   13 20 × 7   14 30 × 7 ...

Use the answers above to work out these divisions.

15 161 ÷ 7   17 469 ÷ 7   19 511 ÷ 7   21 616 ÷ 7

16 378 ÷ 7   18 273 ÷ 7   20 588 ÷ 7   22 644 ÷ 7

Copy and complete these multiplications of 8. Keep going up to 100 × 8.

23 10 × 8   24 20 × 8   25 30 × 8 ...

Use the answers above to work out these divisions.

26 296 ÷ 8   28 440 ÷ 8   30 568 ÷ 8   32 664 ÷ 8

27 368 ÷ 8   29 504 ÷ 8   31 472 ÷ 8   33 760 ÷ 8

○
○ **I am confident with dividing 3-digit numbers by**
○ **1-digit numbers.**

Use the multiples to work out the divisions.

Use these facts
to help you:
$10 \times 6 = 60$
$20 \times 6 = 120$
$30 \times 6 = 180$

Calculate these. Some may have answers with remainders.

1 $84 \div 6 = \square$ **3** $132 \div 6 = \square$ **5** $146 \div 6 = \square$ **7** $187 \div 6 = \square$

2 $88 \div 6 = \square$ **4** $139 \div 6 = \square$ **6** $153 \div 6 = \square$ **8** $206 \div 6 = \square$

Calculate:

9 $10 \times 3 = \square$ **10** $20 \times 3 = \square$ **11** $30 \times 3 = \square$

Calculate these. Some may have answers with remainders.

12 $42 \div 3 = \square$ **14** $69 \div 3 = \square$ **16** $40 \div 3 = \square$ **18** $95 \div 3 = \square$

13 $41 \div 3 = \square$ **15** $64 \div 3 = \square$ **17** $77 \div 3 = \square$ **19** $100 \div 3 = \square$

Divide an even number by an even number. Is the answer always even? Give four examples to explain your answer. Divide an odd number by an odd number. Is the answer always odd? Give four examples to explain your answer.

- I am confident with dividing 3-digit numbers by 1-digit numbers, with remainders.

Calculate:

1 $10 \times 4 = \square$ **2** $20 \times 4 = \square$ **3** $30 \times 4 = \square$ **4** $40 \times 4 = \square$

Use the answers above to work out these divisions.

5 $89 \div 4$ **7** $130 \div 4$ **9** $125 \div 4$ **11** $179 \div 4$

6 $99 \div 4$ **8** $141 \div 4$ **10** $166 \div 4$ **12** $107 \div 4$

Calculate:

13 $10 \times 7 = \square$ **14** $20 \times 7 = \square$ **15** $30 \times 7 = \square$ **16** $40 \times 7 = \square$

Use the answers above to work out these divisions.

17 $155 \div 7$ **19** $237 \div 7$ **21** $306 \div 7$ **23** $317 \div 7$

18 $171 \div 7$ **20** $288 \div 7$ **22** $295 \div 7$ **24** $323 \div 7$

Calculate:

25 $10 \times 8 = \square$ **26** $20 \times 8 = \square$ **27** $30 \times 8 = \square$ **28** $40 \times 8 = \square$

Use the answers above to work out these divisions.

29 $178 \div 8$ **31** $251 \div 8$ **33** $287 \div 8$ **35** $345 \div 8$

30 $199 \div 8$ **32** $276 \div 8$ **34** $330 \div 8$ **36** $364 \div 8$

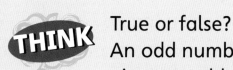 True or false?
An odd number divided by an odd number always gives an odd answer. An even number divided by an even number never gives an odd answer. An even number divided by an odd number always leaves a remainder. An even number divided by 4 never leaves a remainder.

I am confident with dividing 3-digit numbers by 1-digit numbers, with remainders.

Solving word problems

Remember, Rats Never Catch Ants!

Read and try to imagine the story.

Note the information.

Decide what Calculation to do.

Check it makes sense and Answer the problem.

Solve these problems.

1. At a theme park, 183 people are on the Black Hole ride. The ride can hold 238 people. How many more could get on?

2. To go on the Sky ride you must be 135 cm tall. Sam is 107 cm tall. How much more must he grow to be allowed on the ride?

3. On Saturday 2141 people visited the theme park and on Sunday 4863 people visited. How many visited in total on that weekend?

4. 256 people each bought a £4 ticket to go on the Space ride. How much money did they pay altogether?

5. The Giant Wheel has 8 identical pods to carry people. If the wheel can hold 192 people in total, how many can go in each pod?

6. 345 people were on the Corkscrew ride. If 128 people get off and 143 people get on, how many are on the ride now?

7. Two families buy some £7 Picnic Meals. How many meals can they buy for £100? How much change would they get?

8. The Ghost Train had 4856 visitors in one day. If 3035 of them were children, how many more children than adults went on it that day?

I am confident with solving word problems.

Remember, Rats Never Catch Ants!

Read and try to imagine the story.
Note the information.
Decide what Calculation to do.
Check it makes sense and Answer the problem.

Solve these problems.

1. There are 919 passengers at a Greek airport waiting to fly to London, Manchester or Birmingham. 293 are going to London and 368 are going to Manchester. How many are going to Birmingham?

2. On a flight, there are 37 children and 6 times as many adults. How many adults are there?

3. Of the 368 passengers on a plane, 129 are men, 152 are women and the rest are children. How many are children?

4. A plane has 38 rows of seats. Each row has 8 seats. How many seats are there in total?

5. A different plane has 248 seats, of which 67 are empty and 8 are being used by the airline staff. The rest of the seats are taken by passengers. How many passengers are there?

6. On a flight to London, there are 45 children and 4 times as many adults. If there are 293 seats on the plane, how many seats are empty?

7. A plane has 36 rows. The front 10 rows each have 8 seats and the rest of the rows have 10 seats. How many seats are there in total?

I am confident with solving word problems.

Practising calculations

1. $7574 - 800 = \square$

2. $5643 - 50 = \square$

3. $\begin{array}{r} 782 \\ -58 \\ \hline \end{array}$

4. $\begin{array}{r} 977 \\ \times4 \\ \hline \end{array}$

5. $\begin{array}{r} 757 \\ -639 \\ \hline \end{array}$

6. $96 \div 6 = \square$

7. $£975 - £684 = \square$

8. $68 \times 4 = \square$

9. $\frac{5}{8}$ of $40 = \square$

10. $260 \div 5 = \square$

11. $3000 - 2463 = \square$

12. $\begin{array}{r} 5975 \\ +\,7389 \\ \hline \end{array}$

13. $8858 - 450 = \square$

14. $2654 - 440 = \square$

15. $\begin{array}{r} 851 \\ -248 \\ \hline \end{array}$

16. $\begin{array}{r} 369 \\ \times6 \\ \hline \end{array}$

17. $\begin{array}{r} 658 \\ -477 \\ \hline \end{array}$

18. $252 \div 6 = \square$

19. $£539 - £242 = \square$

20. $128 \div 4 = \square$

21. $237 \div 7 = \square$

22. $9763 - 2846 = \square$

23. $6000 - 3439 = \square$

24. $\begin{array}{r} 5875 \\ +\,7276 \\ \hline \end{array}$

25. Mrs Burrow must pay £3·15 in a car park. She puts a £10 note into the machine. How much change should she get?

26. 256 people bought a £4 ticket to go to the cinema. How much money did they pay altogether?

27. There were 7183 men and 3786 women at a rugby match. How many altogether?

cube puzzles

Choose pairs of 3-digit numbers from this cube and find the totals using a written method.

Can you find a pair of numbers:

1 with a total greater than 1000?

2 with a total close to 500?

3 with a total that is a multiple of 10?

4 with a total that has the 10s digit 5?

5 where a digit moves across in all three columns?

6 What is the largest total you can find?

Choose pairs of 3-digit numbers from the cube and find the difference between them using a written method. Can you find a pair of numbers:

7 with a difference less than 100?

8 with a difference close to 500?

9 with a difference that is a multiple of 10?

10 with a difference that has the 10s digit 5?

11 where you must change a 100 into 10s?

Choose a 2-digit number from this cube and multiply it by a 1-digit number using an appropriate written or mental method.

Can you find an answer:

12 that is close to 500?

13 that is a multiple of 10?

14 that is less than 100?

15 using the ladder method, where at least one digit in the addition moves across?

Choose a 2-digit number from the cube above and divide it by a 1-digit number using an appropriate written or mental method. Can you find an answer:

16 that has a remainder of 1?

17 that is an even number?

18 that is greater than 40?

19 that is a multiple of 4?

Choose a 3-digit number from the cube on the left and divide it by a 1-digit number using an appropriate written or mental method.

20 Can you find an answer that is between 40 and 50?

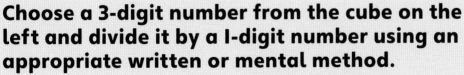

Series Editor
Ruth Merttens

Author Team
Jennie Kerwin and Hilda Merttens

Published by Pearson Education Limited, Edinburgh Gate, Harlow, Essex, CM20 2JE.

www.pearsonschools.co.uk

Text © Pearson Education Limited 2013
Typeset by Debbie Oatley @ room9design
Original illustrations © Pearson Education Limited 2013
Illustrated by Andrew Painter, Matthew Buckley, Marek Jagucki, Debbie Oatley
Cover design by Pearson Education Limited
Cover illustration by Volker Beisler © Pearson Education Limited
Additional contributions by Hilary Koll and Steve Mills, CME Projects Ltd.

First published 2013

16 15 14
10 9 8 7 6 5 4 3 2

British Library Cataloguing in Publication Data
A catalogue record for this book is available from the British Library

ISBN 978 1 408 27851 2

Copyright notice
All rights reserved. No part of this publication may be reproduced in any form or by any means (including photocopying or storing it in any medium by electronic means and whether or not transiently or incidentally to some other use of this publication) without the written permission of the copyright owner, except in accordance with the provisions of the Copyright, Designs and Patents Act 1988 or under the terms of a licence issued by the Copyright Licensing Agency, Saffron House, 6–10 Kirby Street, London EC1N 8TS (www.cla.co.uk). Applications for the copyright owner's written permission should be addressed to the publisher.

Printed in Slovakia by Neografia

Acknowledgements
We would like to thank the staff and pupils at North Kidlington Primary School, Haydon Wick Primary School, Swindon, St Mary's Catholic Primary School, Bodmin, St Andrew's C of E Primary & Nursery School, Sutton-in-Ashfield, Saint James' C of E Primary School, Southampton and Harborne Primary School, Birmingham, for their invaluable help in the development and trialling of this book.

Every effort has been made to contact copyright holders of material reproduced in this book. Any omissions will be rectified in subsequent printings if notice is given to the publishers.